Gron Williams was born in Cardiff, brought up in the pit town of Bargoed, sailed with the wartime RN and graduated at Aberystwyth. He spent 40 years as a daily newspaper staffman, principally in Birmingham and London, before retiring from the *Daily Mail* around the time of the death of Fleet Street. He now lives in Hereford, reports rugby union matches for *The Mail on Sunday*, collects Victorian horse brasses and has an affinity with real ale. He is married and has two daughters.

He has the unquenchable zest of a dash of phosphorus which will blaze anywhere it can find fresh air
— **Manchester Guardian (March 1947)**

FIREBRAND

The Frank Owen Story

Gron Williams

A Square One Publication

First published in 1993 by
Square One Publications
Saga House, Sansome Place, Worcester, WR1 1UA

© Gron Williams 1993

ISBN: 1 872017 75 4

British Library Cataloguing in Publication Data
is available for this book

Typeset by Avon Dataset, Bidford-on-Avon, Warwickshire B50 4JH
Printed in Great Britain by Antony Rowe Ltd, Chippenham, Wiltshire

CONTENTS

FOREWORD

WHEN I retired from the *Daily Mail* to live in Hereford, people kept asking me whether I had known Frank Owen. Had I been there when he was the editor of the *Mail*? Alas, I arrived in London too late for that. I met him briefly a few times but he had long since become yesterday's man. The hot fires had subsided to cold ashes.

But I soon discovered that the legend lived on into the Nineties in his native Hereford. And there were old Fleet Street hands who could recall Frank Owen's meteoric rise and fall.

He was not a figure of historical influence, except perhaps marginally in his contribution to *Guilty Men* which helped topple the Tories in 1945 and in his efforts to build Far East troop morale. But he walked confidently with leaders like Lloyd George, Bevan, Beaverbrook, Mountbatten, Slim and Wingate. His life illuminates many facets of British life we shall not see again, like political hustings, Fleet Street and the hectic business of bringing out a newspaper for hundreds of thousands of British Servicemen exiled on the other side of the world.

1

Many people were generous with anecdotes and information. From press and politics they included Anna Phillips, Michael Foot, Lord (Hugh) Cudlipp, Reg Cudlipp, Sir Edward Pickering, Jeremy Thorpe, Lord (Emlyn) Hooson, Ted Bishop, Denis Brierly, George Elam, Bob Findlay, Jimmy French, Grenville Jones, Jim Nicoll and Tony Pyatt.

In Hereford I was privileged to use the comprehensive political scrapbooks of Doug Hughes whose memories of local hustings were invaluable. Derek Evans recalled the excitement of being a young Liberal in the 1950s. Other local sources were Carol Matthews, Doreen Price, Ted Woodriffe (*Hereford Times*), Steve Carr (*Hereford Journal*), Donald Austins, John Butler, Reg Edwards (Burma Star Association), George Farmer, Lionel Meredith and John Tebbutt.

Rugby stalwarts Harry Bowcott and Johnny Price and *South Wales Argus* veteran Willis Huntley cast light on some early facets of Frank Owen. I was allowed to research the files, cuttings etc of Associated Newspapers, the *Hereford Times*, Hereford Record Office and Hereford Public Library.

I thank Giles, the cartoonist, for allowing me to use the menu cover he drew for the Saints and Sinners Club in 1960, the year Frank Owen was chairman. It makes a superb cover for this book. Other illustrations are by courtesy of Derek Evans, Associated Newspapers and Express Newspapers.

Finally, I dedicate the book to my wife Nell who encouraged me to start it and persevere.

Hereford, July 1993

1. THE FORGOTTEN

We'll meet again, don't know where, don't know
when . . .

Wartime song

IT'S Sunday night and there's a war on. The month is
December, 1944, and hostilities are into their sixth year.
Up and down Britain millions of wireless listeners have
just heard the news and stay tuned in for the Postscript.

Over the weary years they have listened at this time on
the Sabbath to the distinctive and varied voices of the
national morale-boosters: The blunt Yorkshire tones of
J B Priestley; Quentin Reynolds rubbishing Hitler in
robust American; the brisk Canadian of Leonard
Brockington; Philip Joubert's clipped but relaxed Air
Force diction.

Now they hear a new voice full of power and Welsh
border rhetoric but with a bit of American thrown in –
what is nowadays called a Mid-Atlantic accent. Frank
Owen is there to plead the case of South East Asia
Command and in particular General Bill Slim's soldiers
of the 'forgotten' 14th Army soon to start operations on
the Arakan and further north for the reconquest of
Burma. Lord Louis Mountbatten, the Supreme Commander, has sent Owen, his chief publicist and editor of

3

the Command newspaper to tell the British public what is happening East of Suez.

Seated around their meagre coal fires, families listened to Owen's words: 'This is the Burma Front. A quarter of a million British soldiers live there, fight there, march, patrol and stick it out.

'Life is hard on the Burma Front. The true quality of these brave men is that they have overcome all hardships . . . They have built a great military state in the heart of the jungle . . .

'They are the unsung heroes . . . No braver, no finer, prouder, more devoted soldiers have walked this earth.'

The crux of his message was that the Burma troops were prepared for the battles ahead but needed the encouragement and interest of the folks at home. No longer must they be the forgotten.

Frank was having a good war. He had been plucked from the obscurity of second lieutenant in tanks to promotion as Mountbatten's propaganda adviser and editor of the command paper, *SEAC*. He had completed the serious bit of his trip home. Now for the noisy parties with his old Fleet Street mates, stolen hours with his friend, Anna, and a battle with the First Lord of the Admiralty.

Subject of the battle was a young able seaman, Ted Bishop, currently waiting for a ship at Portsmouth Barracks after D-Day service in a destroyer. Whenever he could, he was up the Smoke to moonlight as a journalist on one of the Beaverbrook syndication services. His boss told him: 'You ought to be on a Forces paper. Frank Owen will be home for a trip soon. I'll mention you. You may be lucky.'

Young Ted soon got a message: Go to lunch with

Frank Owen at his Westminster flat. When he got there and asked for the great man, his wife Grace said: 'You'll be lucky. Don't know when he'll be back. But you can have lunch with me.' Frank eventually turned up and said he would fix it for Ted to join him in Calcutta. 'I'll go to see the First Lord of the Admiralty straightaway,' he said.

But A V Alexander, the man who had succeeded Winston Churchill as First Lord, was not obliging. 'I can't spare Bishop,' he said. 'I could let you have a couple of lieutenant-commanders. But we're very short of able seamen.' Frank told Alexander he'd better think again. He was in no awe of politicians, having been an MP himself and a close associate of Lloyd George, Nye Bevan and Max Beaverbrook.

He returned to tell Ted Bishop: 'I'm working on it. We'll get you out there.' Back at Pompey Barracks, the young sailor was piped to see the Commodore who, just one rank below an admiral, is not usually expected to conduct interviews with members of the lower deck.

'It's an extraordinary thing,' said the Commodore. 'I've just had a signal from the First Sea Lord saying you must proceed immediately to India. He doesn't usually get me involved about able seamen. I suppose you must be one of these hush-hush people.'

That was the way big, brash Frank operated, often an irresistible force that shifted even roadblocks. But there was another side to his character. A long sea voyage eventually landed Ted Bishop in Calcutta. He arrived at the *SEAC* newspaper office to find not only that Frank was away up on the Burma Front but that he had made no mention of the new recruit.

The editor in charge said: 'Never heard of you. Don't

want you. Just buzz off back to England.' Ted found a spare bunk and hung on.

'When Frank got back,' said Ted, 'he took one look at me and said: "Where've you been? It took you long enough." I said I thought he should have told somebody. It would have helped.'

If Frank lacked the elephant's proverbial memory, he certainly had the characteristics of another Indian animal. He was as ferocious a tiger as ever came out of the pre-war Fleet Street jungle, fierce in the pursuit of political and social causes, tough on the cubs in his care but a purring pussycat to the ladies, who loved him.

2. TOMMY'S BOY

Frank never ceased to honour his father's
trade

Michael Foot

DYNASTICALLY he was Humphrey Owens III. But he always preferred his second forename and dropped the last letter of his surname in his 20s. So this is the Frank Owen Story, the making of a 20th century Fleet Street editor.

Grandfather Humphrey was a seafaring man, born at Aberystwyth in 1846. The small ports of West Wales were renowned for sending their sons to man the ships of the ever expanding British merchant fleet. When they returned to Aberystwyth, Aberaeron or Aberporth they settled down in cottages which they named after their ships – Hero and Pioneer, Lurline and Afton Stream, Lowther Castle and Crusader – much to the bewilderment of holidaymaking Brummies wandering the streets in later times.

By family tradition they were all sea captains and had sailed the Horn under canvas. Whatever the truth about Humphrey I, he was certainly not without means when he swallowed the anchor and returned to Elizabeth, his Tenby-born wife, and two children. By 1886 he had taken the licence of Number Five Vaults, one of the many public houses in Widemarsh Street, near the centre of Hereford. Soon he moved across the road to the Black Swan, a 'commercial and agricultural hotel'.

The old sailor's son, Thomas Humphrey, was born in 1877, four years before his sister, Annie. In the 1891 Census he is entered as 'scholar' in the 'occupation' column, proving that he was in continued education after the school-leaving age of 13. By that time the Black Swan was prosperous with two live-in servants, Louise Clowes, a Coventry-born barmaid, and house-maid Fanny Jones from Knighton, over the Welsh border.

Thomas Humphrey followed his father's trade and before he was 25 had taken over Number Ten, yet another hostelry in that part of Widemarsh Street near the Hightown. Tommy, ever-enterprising, began bot-tling beer and stout as a wholesale sideline. On November 4, 1905, his son Humphrey Frank was born at the pub, which stood only 20 or 30 yards from David Garrick's birthplace in Maylord Street. They say lightning never strikes twice . . .

Frank's grandfather had meantime retired from the Black Swan and was one of the first to capture the wonder and curiosity of the child. Here were tales of windjammers rounding the Horn, instructions in knot-tying ('You're all thumbs, boy bach. Try again'), ships in bottles to be handled like best china.

This was the world of Captain Cat, the blind sea-dog of *Under Milk Wood*, created and immortalised several decades later by Dylan Thomas. This character in 'the seashelled, ship-in-bottle, shipshape best cabin of

Schooner House' touched a nostalgic nerve when Frank Owen heard the play in the 1950s.

Within a few years the energetic Tommy had retaken the family flagship, the Black Swan, and expanded his bottling activities into large new premises, again in Widemarsh Street. He was the only source of Marston's brews in Hereford and had a reputation for quality mineral waters and squashes.

Now there was a bustling world outside for young Frank to explore. Hereford, a border city since the Middle Ages, was one of the most cosmopolitan centres along the Marches with two main market days and minor markets. The ancient streets teemed with cattle-breeders, Welsh drovers and hill-farmers, Birmingham cattle dealers, cheapjacks and hucksters from the four corners of the kingdom. It had its feuds and border passions. Young Frank insisted he was Welsh and occasionally had to stand up for his nation.

As Frank and his sister, Marjorie Elizabeth, grew up, their mother, who had been Cecily Hannah Green before marriage, became concerned about pub life influences and the Owens family stopped 'living over the shop', moving first to 147 Whitecross Road and later to Wolferlow, a substantial house in Bodenham Road, where doctors, solicitors and the city's shop-keepers of substance abounded.

But before Wolferlow: World War I. Frank was eight when the Allies locked horns with the Kaiser. He was at the age when every schoolboy knew all about Jack Hobbs and Frank Woolley, Fatty Wedlock and Billy Meredith, Jimmy Wilde and Jack Johnson. It was the time of cigarette cards and hero worship.

The war soon took the place of sport in most lads'

minds. Hereford had been a garrison town of sorts for many years, home of the Herefordshire Regiment, a Territorial unit. And there were the Welsh Divisional Transport and Supply Column of the Army Service Corps and the South Wales Mounted Brigade Field Ambulance. The Herefordshires were among those who landed at Suvla Bay in the bloody Gallipoli Campaign.

War was the buzz with late night recruiting meetings in the Hightown to lure well-oiled yokels to the Colours, lapel badges of Kitchener, Jellicoe, French and Haig and threepenny maps at the stationers showing the Western Front. Frank became a student of war and never lost the passion for strategy and weapons.

Midway through the War Frank won a scholarship to Monmouth Grammar School. And Marjorie passed for Monmouth High School. They probably travelled down old railway line to Ross-on-Wye where they changed trains – just over an hour's run.

He made his mark at Monmouth. When he left at 17 he had been rugby skipper, captain of boats and sergeant-major of the Officers Training Corps, in addition to winning a scholarship to Sidney Sussex, the Cambridge college which educated Oliver Cromwell.

A contemporary at Monmouth remembered two things about young Frank – his extraordinarily loud, commanding voice and the fact that he ran an illegal rebel newspaper called *The Red Flag*, not exactly flavour of the month with many people so soon after the Russian Revolution.

It took as its motto some lines from a 17th century dramatist, James Shirley:

Sceptre and crown
Must tumble down,
And in the dust be equal made
With the poor crooked scythe and spade.

Frank produced *The Red Flag* during the Latin lessons out of sight of the master whose very large desk provided protection. But one day they were spotted and it was the cane for the whole subversive editorial board. Frank later told fellow-journalist Tom Driberg: 'We were always getting beaten. It was a choice of a hundred lines or six on the bum. We used to take the six.'

In his early 20s when he was the youngest MP, Frank made a forthright attack on public school disciplinary methods. Writing in the *Daily News*, a Liberal paper, he recalled: 'We pushed games, inter-school and house, to fantastic extremes. We were heartily encouraged by masters with minds no broader than our own – that of boys of 16.

'There was very little flogging but one of the crimes so penalised was the awful one of 'bunking' football. The execution of the sentence frequently fell on the captain of games. He made it plain how painful could be the neglect of duty. I know because I was often executed and later became the executioner.'

These were enlightened views for an ex-public schoolboy in the 1920s and Frank was equally critical of pressures to join the Officers Training Corps.

So to Cambridge with a new motor bike and, in his sights the history tripos and some rugby glory, but apparently little political awareness. The Red Flag had been a red herring.

Frank did lead a three-day sitdown strike but that was a simple protest about poor hall food. He never spoke at the Cambridge Union – in contrast to his slightly younger fellow-Herefordian, Gilbert Harding, whose speech impressed the president (the future Lord Devlin) at a May Week debate.

Indeed, during the General Strike of 1926 Frank Owen, the future rebel of a score of causes, was on the side of the law-abiding middle classes from whom he sprang. According to Driberg, he stoked a Newcastle-bound train which the strikers derailed and then spent his scab's wages drinking with the strikers in their own pubs.

'It's amazing they didn't break our heads,' he said. 'After that I began to think and to identify myself with the workers in argument.'

But this was no red-hot instant conversion on the road to Damascus. Frank lived the good student life – studying hard and playing hard, downing his ale, rowing for his college and chasing a rugby blue.

It was a vintage time for Cambridge sport. The British athletics team in the 1924 Paris Olympics included 16 Light Blues who brought back two golds (Harold Abrahams and Douglas Lowe), a silver and three bronzes. The cricket eleven in Frank Owen's time included Percy Chapman, Leonard Crawley, New Zealander Tom Lowry, Maurice Turnbull, Walter Robins and the graceful Indian, Prince Duleepsinhji, who in May 1927 hit 254 not out in four hours off the Middlesex bowling.

But rugby glory evaded Frank. Not once did he play in the December Twickenham fixture against Oxford which is the only qualification for a Blue. Harry

*Frank in the 1924–25 Hereford rugby XV, flanked by Captain
C H Geake and Dr R Wood-Power.*

Bowcott, a Welsh international centre who was up at
Cambridge just after Owen but played frequently
alongside him for London Welsh, explained: 'Frank
had a number of matches for the Varsity. He was
powerful centre, straight-running, hard-tackling.

'But competition for back positions was very hot in
his years. We had future Welsh internationals like Rowe
Harding, Windsor Lewis and Guy Morgan. In addition
there were the England men, Carl Aarvold, Sir Thomas
Devitt and T E S Francis.'

Frank was playing for Hereford during vacations and
had also joined London Welsh. He was good enough to
play in two Welsh National trials in the autumn of 1926,

13

in particular distinguishing himself for the Anglo-Welsh against the Probables at Bridgend on November 26. But he was unable to match the ability of the 19-year-old John Roberts and a Cambridge colleague, Lou Turnbull, in the other centre positions.

Rugby continued after Owen's Cambridge days. He turned out for Newport while working there for the *South Wales Argus* and returned to London Welsh to become possibly the only sitting MP to play first-class rugby.

In the summer of 1927 Frank Owen left Cambridge with first-class honours in part 2 of the history tripos after a superior second-class in part 1 the previous year. His special study had been the American Civil War. He had been head-hunted for the Indian Civil Service, but after due consideration he turned that down. He was restive and sought the adventure of newspaper journalism.

Frank's father, known to customers and friends as Tommy Owens, was a man of substance in Hereford. When his son came home at the age of 22 with first-class honours he was proud, basking in the reflected glory, as is natural for such a fortunate parent.

But Tommy was very much aware that Frank was his own man – determined to carve out a turbulent career in the wider world.

He had a charisma and an animal magnetism that pulled the girls. He boozed with relish, meanwhile arguing politics loudly and cogently late into the night. Tommy was no man to take a tiger by the tail. He stood back and reflected what a handful he and Cecily had unleashed on the world.

Tommy Owens was a typical provincial entrepreneur

of his time, shrewd and willing to take a risk. There were more than a hundred licensees in Hereford in his time but he was the one with the enterprise to open a bottling store and make it a little goldmine. He recruited his syrup-mixer – a skilled operative on whom the success of soft drinks rested – from Oxford and set him up in Hereford.

His hobby was coursing and the fraternity held their meetings at the Black Swan. He raced greyhounds under GRA rules, most notably Tall Oaks which had notable successes before Tommy sold him for £27.6s. in 1927.

Skullduggery struck soon afterwards when Tall Oaks was one of six dogs who died mysteriously at their Belle Vue kennels in Manchester. The trainer was banned because the dogs had been accidently poisoned by the administration of illegal stimulants. Another of the dead animals, Turned Out, still belonged to Tommy, who brushed aside comments about guilt by association and carried on running his dogs. He did it his way – as did Frank.

3. ASSORTED WIZARDS

The wise, far-seeing electors of my native
Hereford sent me to Westminster and two
years later in 1931 the lousy bastards kicked
me out—

Frank Owen

FRANK OWEN hit the *Argus* newsroom like a rooster in a
dovecote. The senior reporters, six quizzical pro-
fessionals with fingers on all the pulses of the Welsh
coal centre of Newport, looked with tolerant scepticism
on the flamboyant new boy just down from Cambridge.

But the only junior journalist on the *South Wales
Argus*, Willis Huntley, was perhaps more impressed.
Looking back 65 years, he said: 'I remember a big chap.
Quick tempered. Very certain of himself with a loud
voice. He came to us for the experience. He wasn't paid
at the start. Only expenses. Our complement was full.
Seven reporters, including me, the apprentice, and four
sub-editors. The *Argus* was run on a shoestring in the
late Twenties.'

Huntley recalls that Owen made his reputation with a
series of articles about the Forest of Dean which had its
recession problems like all the coalfields in those days.
Eventually he was put on the payroll. Things brightened
up in other directions. He joined the local lecture

circuit, addressing Rotary clubs and the like in South-East Wales and the border towns right up to Hereford.

Frank was well-equipped to talk about international affairs. He had spent the long summer Varsity vacations in Geneva attending sessions of the League of Nations. He was nominally employed by an Australian news agency but this was on a 'stringer' basis. They paid only for the copy they used. So, just as in the initial days at Newport, the family finances from the Hereford bottling plant took the strain.

These were the heady, optimistic days of the League, days of the belief in collective security and the efficiency of sanctions, of the Locarno Treaty and disarmament talks. Frank was good value on his feet, fluent and forthright. His paper, the *Argus*, was staunchly Liberal, founded in 1892 by Sir Garrod Thomas, a consultant physician, to promote the cause of the party.

And Frank, who in 1926 had rallied round to help break the National Strike, became in two years a radical behind the banner of David Lloyd George. He began speaking for the party, travelling up to the Pontypool constituency to support Captain Geoffrey Crawshay, a man of remarkably varied talents. This tall ex-Guards officer was a sprig of the famous Merthyr iron-founding family. He established his own rugby touring team, chaired the Welsh Board of Health, founded a contemporary arts society and became herald bard of the National Eisteddfod Gorsedd.

Another of Crawshay's activities was to hold breakfasts for Welshmen in residence at Oxford and Cambridge. They became a tradition of the academic year. It was undoubtedly at one of these that Frank Owen – always proud of being Welsh – met the Captain, who could well have given the young man an introduction to both the Garrod Thomas paper and the Liberal Party.

Soon we find Frank on the Press table of the Welsh Liberal conference at Aberystwyth. He volunteered to make the traditional valedictory speech for the correspondents, Lloyd George heard him, was impressed and asked him round to breakfast next day.

The old Welsh Wizard had spotted a sorcerer's apprentice. He offered Frank a place on his political staff. The offer was at first turned down but later the young journalist moved to London to take a £5-a-week job in the Lloyd George 'think tank'. Though somewhat discredited and at odds with both his old Tory allies and many of his fellow-Liberals, Lloyd George was not a spent force – and he commanded substantial party funds. He itched to be Prime Minister again. The man who had won the war fancied his chance of solving the problems of unemployment and slump.

Since his Coalition government collapsed in 1922, the old fox from Criccieth had been working for the opportunity he thought was golden when Stanley Baldwin called an election for May 1, 1929. Lloyd George had control of substantial party funds which his enemies said were built up by the sale of honours and titles. Lord Rosebery called it 'a prostitution of the Royal Prerogative'.

Whatever the rights and wrongs of this, Lloyd George was certainly in funds. He could employ bright young men like Frank Owen to research and present the Liberal policies. He could put 512 candidates in the field with 615 seats at stake. The party were strong on propaganda with an outstanding poster and advertising campaign. And they had a clear policy for fighting unemployment. It was Keynesian, forerunner of the prime-the-pump New Deal which Roosevelt used to revive the United States a few years later.

Frank had a big part in writing the master plan which envisaged putting 350,000 to work on roads and bridges, 60,000 on housebuilding and so on up to a total of 586,000 new jobs in the first year and another 600,000 in the second. The young man explained: 'These plans will not add a penny to taxation. Their cost will be met by the saving in unemployment benefit and the increase in revenue from improved rates.'

The Liberal candidate for Hereford was to have been Major F M Dougall, a DFC with the Royal Flying Corps in World War I. He pulled out with six weeks to go before the election. Ill health was the official reason but he was reckoned not to have much chance in a division which had been Tory since 1893.

Frank Owen, on a mission for the party in Cornwall, was offered the vacancy and without hesitation came like young Lochinvar out of the West to fight Hereford at the age of 23.

Tommy came in the car to meet him at the station. 'Heard about the election?' he asked Frank. 'The Liberals have put up some youngster. Still wet behind the ears.'

'I've got news for you, Dad. I'm the candidate'.

For Tory candidate Eric Romilly it must have seemed like taking candy from a kid. He already had one no-hope opponent, Labour's Henry Cooper, a Boer War and Great War soldier who ran a Park Lane dancing school where he had taught the Prince of Wales (later Edward VIII) to foxtrot. Fame indeed!

But Frank was no pushover. He was a local boy. He was politically sophisticated beyond his years thanks to

Cambridge, Geneva, the *Argus* and Lloyd George. He spoke loud and clear, declaiming his radical beliefs from the heart. No mumbling upper middle class inhibitions here. A Boanerges of the hustings calling down fire to consume his Conservative opponents.

Locals buzzed with a piece of Owen repartee worthy of his mentor, Lloyd George. At an early-campaign meeting in the cattle market, a Methodist minister told the candidate: 'I am a Liberal but I could never vote for a man who was born in a public house.' Frank was in like a flash: 'Wasn't Jesus Christ born in a pub? You'd vote for him, wouldn't you?'

And there was the flapper factor. Until 1928 the women's vote had been confined to those over 30. Now it included those from 21 upwards. Add to this a young Adonis with a Hollywood profile and it is no surprise the young ladies of Hereford flocked to his colours. Frequently at Frank's side was Mary Edwards, a good-looker whom many thought he would marry. And his sister, Marjorie, led an active troupe of feminine canvassers.

Came polling day and the shock result:

F. Owen (Lib)	14,208
E. Romilly (Con)	13,087
H Cooper (Lab)	1,901
Majority	1,121

Panic at the declaration on the steps of the Shire Hall. No winning candidate present to propose the customary vote of thanks to the presiding officer. Romilly did his grudging best to deputise but not without the audible aside, 'Hereford has gone mad'.

Frank turned up late (delayed by dalliance at

*Frank addresses
the 1929 Hereford
election victory
rally from the
back of a van in
Widemarsh Street.
His father's pub,
the Black Swan, is
on the right.*

Ledbury, they said) and was carried on a chair of triumph down Union Street.

His opponents had a petty revenge. They made his father, Tommy, unwelcome at the Conservative Club where he had been a member for years and took the club's custom away from the Owens bottling store. 'Tommy hadn't raised a finger in public to support his boy,' said one ancient Herefordian. 'It was a bit unkind.'

The youngest member of the House of Commons, the new Member for Hereford, was one of only 59 Liberals. Lloyd George had hoped for 250. Instead it was Labour with 287 seats who had become the undisputed radical standard-bearers. Among the other new MPs were Lloyd George's daughter, Megan, who was 27, and the impassioned socialist daughter of a Scots miner, Jenny Lee, who at 24 was just a year older than Frank.

But the newcomer who made the biggest impact was Nye Bevan (later to marry Jenny Lee). This 32-year-old ex-miner from Tredegar completed Frank's tripos in Welsh magic. The sorcerer's apprentice had met Crawshay who walked with druids and knew the ways of influence. He had worked for Lloyd George, the wizard of rhetoric and manipulation. Now came Bevan, an enchanter with words, a spellbinder, capable of impaling a political enemy with a phrase.

When Bevan died in 1960 Frank Owen wrote an obituary in the *Daily Express* which contained one of the very best pieces of folksy autobiography he ever published. He tells how he first met Bevan:

'I was then a young reporter on the *South Wales Argus* and had been sent up the valley to Tredegar where Nye was a member of the Urban District Council . . . My memories endure of the vehement, yes

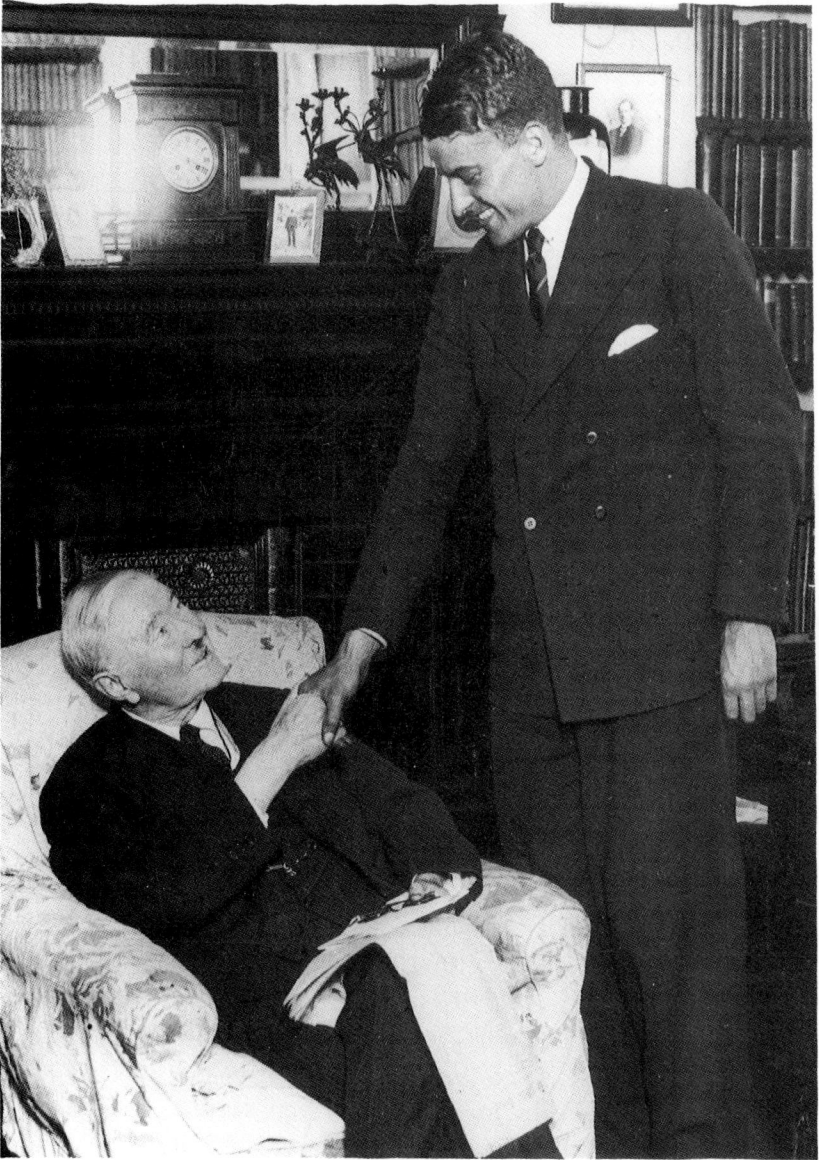

The 'father' of the Commons, T P O'Connor, greets the 'baby' of the House, H F Owen.

vitriolic, outbursts of the dynamic speaker.

'I was returned myself as a young Liberal MP to the same House of Commons as Nye in 1929 . . . On a number of issues, especially unemployment – and the utter, tragic failure of Ramsay MacDonald's Labour Government to tackle it – Nye and I shared the same opinion. We became close friends and within a year or two we were sharing the same flat.

'It was in a mews above a garage off the Cromwell Road, Kensington. Small, two-bedroomed with living and dining room, kitchen and bathroom. Rent: £2 a week. Neither of us had much money beyond our MP's salary (then £400 a year). And we sometimes forgot when the rent was due.

'But not for long! Because acting for the person who had rented us the flat was another friendly (Tory!) MP. He sometimes reminded each of us as we sat or stood listening to the debate. And, as the story went, whichever one of us it was he tackled would reply in astonishment: 'What! Hasn't old – – – sent off the cheque yet?'

'A later legend ran that once he tracked both of us together into the same voting lobby (and found himself supporting the Labour Government).'

Frank describes the flat: 'Enter the narrow front door, climb the stairs and turn right for the living-dining room. Owen's own little room was also on the right and was on top of the noisy garage. Socialist Bevan's room was on the left – and it was a much larger one, although beyond his windows there was a railway. Nye always insisted it was even noisier.

'Halfway up the staircase a fine pair of antlers decorated the wall. Nye invented a story about them. He said we reached an agreement not to disturb one another. If he wished to be left alone, he would hang his hat on the left antler. If I wished to be left alone, I would hang mine on the right antler. "We lived there for more than a year," said Nye, "and by the time we left those antlers had been worn down to a couple of thumbs." I had to spoil his story by pointing out that in those days I never wore a hat. Nye did.

'But this side of the tale is true: We would argue on long into the night and even until the dawn came up. When we parted I went off to sleep. Nye would start reading. And when I was ready for breakfast he would be reading still.'

Jenny Lee, recalling in post-war years the hilarious Cromwell Road days, says of Frank: 'There was no tortuous neurosis about that charming companion. He was full of the joys of spring in an honest-to-God, straightforward way.' He charmed them all.

Frank Owen made his biggest impact on the Commons in 1931 when he moved the adjournment of the house to protest the imprisonment of a youth from his constituency who was accused of poaching.

A sentence of three months had been passed on 18-year-old Alfred Charles Jones from the village of Abbeydore. He was charged before Hereford magistrates with stealing a pheasant.

The young MP pitched his plea dramatically: 'I want to enlist support on behalf of a free citizen of this country who has been the subject of a violation of the elementary principles of justice as flagrant and as scandalous as anything that may have disgraced the Russian Revolution. It is a case of feudal domination in an English village amounting to a gross interference

27

with and subversion of the course of justice.'

Jones and a 30-year-old companion, George Payne, were appearing under the 1828 Night Poaching Act when the chairman of magistrates was called out of court to talk with the landowner on whose estate the pheasant had been taken. The case proceeded until the police pointed out that the chairman was absent. When the case was resumed the chairman sent the 18-year-old to Gloucester Gaol for three months and fined the older defendant who had 'been led astray' by Jones.

Frank, who had received a 500-signature petition supporting the youth, called the sentence 'harsh and savage'. The Speaker ruled that the phrase was out of order and Frank's late night filibuster looked to be over until Lloyd George intervened, saying it was the Lord Chancellor's duty to deal with a magistrate who left the court to confer with a party to the case.

The Home Office climbed down and the Secretary of State, J R Clynes, reconsidered the case. Jones, who had already been in gaol two months, was released.

Frank also won a battle on the floor of the House to preserve Broadmoor Common at Fownhope near Hereford. These were fights against the local gentry reminiscent of Lloyd George's own early crusades as a local solicitor making his way up the ladder to become a populist MP.

The Hereford constituency was carefully nursed by its young Member, often even with decorum, as when he turned up in morning dress to become the godfather of Margaret Cratchley at her christening. She was the daughter of the Owens Bottling Store office manager.

Nationally, Frank's most important Commons speech was an attack on Sir Oswald Mosley in a debate of October 1930. Mosley, sixth baronet, educated Winchester, Sandhurst and the trenches, had started political life as a Tory but moved across to Labour. He had, with Jimmy Thomas and George Lansbury, been called up by Premier Ramsay MacDonald to form the unlikely trinity which was to conquer unemployment. They failed and Mosley marched out of the Government though staying in the Labour Party.

In the debate on the Address Sir Oswald expressed views that were shortly to lead him to create the British Fascist party. Frank Owen accused him of preaching 'the crudity of economic nationalism' and the 'barbarity of economic isolation'. Such jingoism would lead to 'a new and more frightful world conflict'. Frank's speech was much admired.

A trip to Russia in the following May and June to advance the young MP's knowledge of world politics was hardly over before crisis engulfed the Government. MacDonald deserted his party to preside over a National administration consisting of a few Labour cronies, the Conservative Party and the majority of the Liberals.

A general election followed in the October. Lloyd George was left leading a rump of six candidates. Frank was one of them. Mrs Doreen Price (nee Morrish) tells the story: 'I was Frank Owen's constituency secretary during the 1931 election. A telegram arrived from Sir John Simon, leader of the National Liberals asking him to support the National Coalition. Frank said: "Certainly not. I went in as a radical Liberal under Lloyd George and that is what I remain."

If Frank had followed Simon, he would have held Hereford because the Conservatives would have stood down their candidate. Striking out against the tide cost him dear. The girls of Marjorie Owen's Young Liberal dancing troupe again worked their hearts out for Frank but the national landslide buried him.

In the event Hereford Tories found a very adequate candidate who was to represent them for almost 25 years – J P L Thomas, a future First Lord of the Admiralty. Voting was on October 27 and the figures were:

J. Thomas (Con)	19,418
F. Owen (Lib)	12,465
Majority	6,953

Lloyd George was left leading a family foursome of Independent Liberals: Himself, son Gwilym, daughter Megan and Goronwy Owen, Gwilym's brother-in-law. Frank Owen was one of their two casualties. The other was Edgar Wallace, prolific writer of thrillers, racing novels and film scripts. This one-time Fleet Street hack had contested Blackpool.

Frank Owen picked himself up, dusted himself down and immediately adjusted his sights a mile further down the Thames from Westminster to Fleet Street. One wry flash of repartee revealed the hurt of rejection. Michael Foot recalls how Frank would occasionally declaim: 'The wise, far-seeing, independent electors of Hereford sent me to Westminster and two years later the lousy bastards kicked me out.'

4. BEAVERING

Give them stardust —
Daily Express Editor Arthur Christiansen

FRANK had played the rebel in the Commons. Curiously the radical press made him no offers. The Liberal *News Chronicle*, for whom he had written a much-praised series of articles from Russia while an MP, and the Labour *Daily Herald* were not interested. But Lord Beaverbrook's quirky but basically Tory *Daily Express* certainly was.

This, in any case, was the paper for an ambitious journalist to join, brash, self-confident, abrasive, tuned to the optimistic mood of the rising, surburban middle class. One had only to look at the new *Express* office halfway up Fleet Street with its towering, black glass facade, the menacing castle of a sinister little baron, to know that here was a daily sheet determined to eclipse all rivals. Beaverbrook had completed the building in 1931 not long before Frank Owen was recruited.

Fleet Street had been the home of 'the Print' since 1500 when Wynkyn de Worde set up his first press there. A century and a half later the Great Fire of London raged thereabouts, engulfing the Cheshire Cheese tavern which was rebuilt in 1667 and patronised by Dr Samuel Johnson in the following century.

But the Street as a 20th Century phenomenon did not begin to take shape until the inspired and unstable Alfred Harmsworth (later Lord Northcliffe) created the first popular national sheet, the *Daily Mail*, in 1896. The *Express* followed four years later and the *Daily Mirror* in 1903. None of them started on Fleet Street but were to be found in side streets a few minutes walk from the thoroughfare.

In 1909 Philip Gibbs (later to be knighted as a distinguished 1914 – 18 war correspondent) wrote a best-selling novel called *The Street of Adventure* describing life on a national newspaper.

Francis Luttrell, shy, sensitive son of a rural rector, is thrown in at the deep end. He joins the reporting staff of *The Rag* and is confronted by a whole gallimaufry of initially frightening characters – the hard-bitten crime reporter, the bully boy news editor, the West End stage gossip-monger with a penchant for chatting up barmaids, the gangling man of fashion chasing aristocrats for stories and borrowing half-sovereigns from colleagues who are seldom paid back, and the lady reporter whose cynicism shocks the rector's boy.

They work all hours for a pittance, are exposed to the seamy side of London life, get thrown out of their jobs, often turn to drink. The story is mawkish for modern tastes, full of high-minded Edwardian sentiment and abounds with excruciating Cockney-speak from the lower orders. But this was a novel that 'sold' to the British public a Fleet Street legend which lasted until almost the end of the century when modern technology and the industrial defeat of the print unions fragmented the business to the four corners of Central London.

The House that Max built — Fleet Street's black palace, completed 1931

So when Frank Owen arrived for his first day on the *Express* he was joining a picaresque profession to whose traditions he would quickly conform. His new employer was a remarkable fisher of men. His Canadian lordship was capable of hiring bizarre figures for his newspaper group, like the feckless Irish peer, Castlerosse, who was employed to write society gossip, and Michael Wardell, captain of Hussars, friend of the Prince of Wales, one-eyed with a black pirate patch, whom Beaverbrook made managing director of the *Evening Standard*.

Apart from such cronies, he eagerly recruited and promoted youthful journalistic talent. Among the early young lions was Percy Cudlipp, eldest of three remark-able Cardiff brothers. He edited the *Evening Standard* at 27 but quit to take over the *Daily Herald* after a few years because he could not stand the autocratic Wardell breathing down his neck. By July 1933 when the red crusader first appeared alongside the *Daily Express* masthead, Arthur Christiansen (assistant editor), Frank Owen (leader writer), William Barkley (political corre-spondent) and Gordon Beckles (feature writer) repre-sented flaming youth on the paper.

Owen and Christiansen hit it off from the start. It was a friendship of contrasts between men who was each to put his individual cachet on the job of editor: Arthur the king of lay-out and display; Frank the thunderer of ideas and opinions. Christiansen wrote many years later of how they became inseparable and frequently went on the town after the last edition had gone to press, arguing with fellow-journalists and bandying wisecracks with the satellites of cafe society.

He recalled: 'Once we signed our names on the plaster cast of Peggy Hopkins Joyce, the much-married lovely who had broken her leg ski-ing and who became quite a friend of ours. But mostly we drank a little and dreamed dreams, unless some drunk like poor Robert Newton, the actor, made a nuisance of himself, in which case he first got a warning and then a sockeroo from Frank.' These twin spirits sometimes quarrelled bitterly, particularly about Frank's unpunctuality close to edition time, though never did he fail to catch the press with his powerful leaders. Christiansen concluded: 'I do not know whether I taught him anything but he certainly taught me plenty about politics, about people, about life.'

It was a heady experience being a newspaper writer. Until radio and TV news became more than basic information services, Fleet Street was the prime medium not only of news but of the nation's topical opinion making, background knowledge and cultural entertainment. In those days people would say: 'It must be true: I read it in the paper.' Political commentators like A J Cummings, columnists Hannen Swaffer and Cassandra (Bill Connor), sportswriters Trevor Wignall and Peter Wilson; they all counted.

But there was a flipside to Fleet Street. It was a land of hostelries from the high profile El Vino's to the pocket handkerchief Auntie's near the *Mail*, from the bumpy wooden floors of the antique Cheshire Cheese to the long bar of the Kings and Keys. One could – and often did – become a legend in one's lunchtime (in a phrase that long preceded the satirical magazine *Private Eye*). And in this free-rolling society of easy friendships and lavish expense sheets there was scope for a lot of casual bed-hopping and more permanent arrangements.

It was a world made for Frank Owen, dedicated

35

professional, opinionated student of politics and economics with a machine gun flow of ideas and words . . .
and lusty too. He could earn his corn and sow his oats.
He certainly played hard. This burly 6ft 2in innkeeper's
son could absorb his booze. And his Hollywood profile
attracted women. While Chelsea had its bright young
things, there were plenty of liberated ladies around Fleet
Street. One was discovered dying in Frank's bed,
causing a rare trauma in his life.

Patsy, 28-year-old wife of an *Express* colleague, had
gone to live with Frank at his Bury Walk flat off the
Fulham Road in Chelsea. On the night of November 25,
1934, they went to a party. She left in a huff about 4am.
Frank arrived home 15 minutes later to find her semi-
conscious in bed. Her bottle of sleeping tablets,
previously half-full, contained only four, Frank told the
coroner. She died in hospital.

Patsy's husband, Gordon, gave evidence that his wife
had been living with Frank but no divorce proceedings
were pending. The tablets had been prescribed for
sleeplessness during a trip to Berlin the previous year.
Patsy had been an impulsive person.

Pathologist Sir Bernard Spilsbury said Patsy died in a
coma following poisoning by one of the Veronal group
of drugs. The coroner, unable to decide whether the
taking of such a quantity of the drug was deliberate or
accidental, recorded an open verdict.

Frank Owen was heartbroken. Beaverbrook came to
his aid, gave him a room in Stornoway House, his West
End residence, and 'fussed him like a father', according
to Christiansen.

The tragedy spelled the end of Frank's political
ambitions for 20 years. The news hit Hereford electors

like a depth charge. It was one thing to nudge a fellow-Liberal and joke that the prospective candidate was a bit of a lad with the ladies. But this scandal was much too strong stuff for provincial moral attitudes. Loaded words like 'Chelsea' and 'Veronal' belonged in Evelyn Waugh novels about the flapper set. In February, 1935, Frank wrote to tell the city's Liberal Association he would not be standing next time. He trusted they would understand.

This was soon after his return from a trip to South America with Beaverbrook, Castlerosse and the great man's mistress, Jean Norton, among others. He had established himself as Beaverbrook's personal 'voice', sometimes ghost writer, sometimes contributor of major articles under his own by-line, in addition to his role as the *Daily Express* chief leader writer. Christiansen had already become at 29 editor of that paper but he was merely the man who — albeit brilliantly — brought out the editions. Frank Owen was the creative writer who honed, refined and added bite to his proprietor's thoughts. And Beaverbrook, the great propagandist, valued that talent most.

An American flavour characterised Frank's leader-writing. In the past unsigned editorials had been long ponderous pieces of polemic, erudite essays for the leisured, educated man. Owen's 'Opinion' column threw all this out of the window. In came brief, punchy, snappy comments. Sentences were short. So were words. There was no ambiguity. Fifty years on, it is the style known as 'tabloid English'. And interestingly, such writing owes not a little to the 1611 King James authorised version of the Bible.

Beaverbrook, whose dynamic was both beneficial

and mischievous in two world wars and a campaign to sustain the British Empire, treated Frank Owen like a wayward, headstrong son. Once in the early days his lordship was walking through one end of the editorial floor when he heard someone bellowing into the phone at the other. 'Who's that noisy sod?' asked the boss.

'It's Frank Owen talking to New York office,' replied a minion.

'Why the hell doesn't he use the telephone?' grumbled Beaverbrook.

The Canadian was a lavish host. Stornoway House, stoutly sentried by valet Albert, was the regular haunt of journalists, politicians, trade union bosses, film stars and free-loaders. Bob Findlay, later to be sports editor of the *Daily Express*, *Daily Sketch* and *Daily Mail*, describes one hectic evening: 'I first met Frank Owen at a Beaverbrook Christmas party at Stornoway House. Frank knocked out the butler in a drunken fracas. In addition, Frank Waters, a Scottish rugby international, peed through the open window, Jim Fairley, a *Sunday Express* feature writer, died in a taxi on the way home and Lord Beaverbrook was somewhat miffed when a sports hack bent his ear with an earnest plea to make Page One the main sports page.'

The house guests who attended upon his lordship at Cherkley, his country seat near Leatherhead, were more select. Apart from men on his payroll like Castlerosse, Wardell and Owen, Beaverbrook invited a wide variety of people, including Nye Bevan, German Ambassador Ribbentrop, Churchill protege Brendan Bracken and dramatist Frederick Lonsdale. Attendance at the lord's manor established Frank's place in the pecking order but he was always happier carousing round Fleet Street and the West End.

One of his favourite watering holes was Frisco's in Soho. Frisco himself was from Santo Domingo, a negro who presided over the revels in white tie, tails and top hat and often led his clients in a conga-style line. It was called trucking then. Frank, a man of simple pleasures, enjoyed telling Frisco stories – of how, after being burgled, the gravel-voiced night club owner said sadly: 'They got away with all my passports.'

On another occasion, one of the night club girls shot her lover on the premises during working hours. The C.I.D. arrived to find all the clients had faded away into the gloom and the only likely witness a debutante who had passed out under her table. Frank would recount how she looked up coyly at the detective and said: 'The only shots I heard were the click, click, click of the hypodermics.' Guy Burgess, the spy, apparently relished the same anecdote.

Entertainers from across the Atlantic fascinated the smart set of the Thirties who danced to the beat of Carroll Gibbons and Roy Fox, applauded the crooning of Hutch and the minstrel humour of Scott and Whaley. Frank Owen was following this trend when he began to affect an American accent. And, when he married later in the decade, it was to a showgirl from the States.

How did Frank Owen strike his older colleagues? One acute observer was Trevor Wignall, a fellow-Welshman. He had campaigned in the Boer War with the 3rd Glamorgan Rifle Volunteers and returned to work as a journalist in his native Swansea. Wignall went on to become Fleet Street's first sports columnist,

Trevor Wignall
(drawn by Sava for the Sunday Referee)
Bob Findlay (in foreground)

blazing a trail on the *Express* for such writers as John McAdam, Henry Rose and Des Hackett.

He told in his autobiography how he was asked 'to bid welcome to a tallish, dark-haired, stalwart youngster who was the possessor of the only eyes I ever really saw flash. His hands were in his pockets, but I felt at a glance that they would be out in a jiffy if anybody in the company spoke out of turn.'

The older journalist decided he had met a 'born rebel with the tail of his coat continually trailing'. This would be a useful customer to have on one's side in a brawl.

'Where'er he walked there was commotion and ribaldry and blasphemy,' wrote Wignall. 'But he was a lovable cove even when his fists were flying . . . and he was more loyal than loyalty itself. And he was a simply terrific writer. How he composed his pieces was a mystery. He would sprawl over his desk, shout and yell even when his pen was moving, and would frequently quarrel with his inkwell before lifting his tousled head.

'The idea of chopping leaders into smallish paragraphs was known before he was out of school, but it required his coming to impress editors with the certainty that the short leader, with its clipped phrases, was easier to read and far easier to recollect than the ponderous essays of those who had lived long before his day.'

Wignall, who had known all the great Fleet Street figures like Edgar Wallace, Charlie Hands and Hannen Swaffer, found an exclusive category for Frank Owen. He could say more, and say it more finely, in ten lines than his predecessors could have said in a column.

5. HIS MASTER'S VOICE

I ran the paper purely for the purposes of
making propaganda —

Beaverbrook

FROM the time Frank Owen became *Daily Express* chief
leader writer he was paid to follow the Beaverbrook
line, a contracted hitman with verbal bullets aimed at
targets the paymaster indicated. That was the theory
and it was generally followed until . . .

When the dictators, Hitler and Mussolini began
throwing their weight about, Beaverbrook took up the
fashionable appeasement line. It probably made political sense to him, while some of his friends, like Sir
Samuel Hoare, were leading players of the policy.

A large section of the British public sympathised with
Abyssinia (now Ethiopia) when in the autumn of 1935
Mussolini's Italians invaded that African country whose
Emperor went into genteel exile with his family at Bath.
Beaverbrook swam against the tide and with the
Establishment, writing personally-signed articles (prob-
ably phrased and polished by Owen) which favoured
letting Mussolini off the hook of international action.

Yet his lordship allowed Frank to write at least one
leader supporting the League of Nations sanctions

policy, just as he permitted the combative, left wing, New Zealand-born cartoonist, Low, to savage the jut-jawed Italian dictator in the pages of the *Evening Standard.*

Again, when the dictators gave blatant aid to Franco in the Spanish Civil War, Frank was allowed to support pro-Republican intervention in opposition to Government policy. Years later, he recalled: 'I asked to go to Spain and report what I saw. When I did that, Beaverbrook printed it – and it was certainly no plea for non-intervention.'

The ventriloquist and the dummy were, however, on the same wavelength about the Abdication of December, 1936. Beaverbrook belonged to the King's party who, including Churchill, were those prepared to see Edward VIII marry Wallis Simpson as long as she did not become Queen – what is called a morganatic marriage. This would have allowed the King to be crowned without consort the following May.

Frank was in the thick of the fray and the *Express* thought a settlement had been negotiated when Mrs Simpson offered to take a back seat marriage. Editor Christiansen gives a graphic description of how he, Frank, Tom Driberg and others had a crazy party at Frisco's when the last edition had gone to bed at 2.30 am. Came the dawn and the realisation that the Establishment – Prime Minister Baldwin, the Church and *The Times* – had refused the compromise, forcing Edward to choose abdication.

Work started immediately in the *Daily Express* building on an Abdication book. The joint-authors were Frank Owen and Reg Thompson, phlegmatic, pipe-smoking assistant editor. He made an admirable foil to the fiery Welshman. The book was completed in a weekend but not published until the following March.

The 'remarkable double role' of the Press is closely analysed – first the open and universal conspiracy to write nothing about the King's affair with Mrs Simpson while the rest of the world's newspapers were running it at great length. Once the cat was out of the bag in Britain, however, the authors noted how fiercely the anti-Simpson newspapers conducted their campaign to force Edward to give up either his mistress or his throne.

That was the high politics of the issue but very much more graphic is the chapter (clearly written by Frank) about Edward's tour of South Wales – a slump-stricken coal mining area – a few weeks before the Abdication. He writes: 'The King travelled overnight and woke in a railway siding . . . South Wales hung out their banners and their brave rags to cheer the man who had been their Prince for 25 years. Five times the police cordons were broken. It started in Pontypridd. In Merthyr, police, ex-servicemen and ambulance workers joined hands vainly against the delirious crowds. In Aberdare 20,000 people surged about the King's car and sang till they were hoarse.

'In one village the King stepped from his car and looked on the scene of desolation: long, twisted pipes, rusting engines, broken-down pit-head gear, grass growing over the slag; and he stepped back appalled and deeply moved . . . the tension was broken by a group of voices lifted up into the hymn 'Crug-y-Bar', a Welsh dirge that begins with a wail and ends on a note of triumph . . .

'At the end of the long day, after a 60 miles tour, the King passed by the night shift at Abercwmboi, just going down. They waved their miners' lamps in the dusk. Edward was profoundly affected. 'Something will be done for you,' he said, a message that will be remembered long after the valedictory denunciations of the Archbishops are forgotten . . .

'A fortnight later, when it was all over, a stunned and sullen South Wales received the news that the King had gone. Some said: "They pushed him out because he tried to help us." More bitterly others: "We've been used".'

That Christmas in the Valleys the carol-singing urchins revelled in a parody: 'Hark the herald angels sing, Mrs Simpson stole our King.' But the rampaging Fascists of Europe quickly drove this royal crisis out of the headlines.

Beaverbrook and Churchill had been among the King's men battling to save Edward, but the pair were far from united about Hitler.

Churchill had a contract to write for the *Standard* and naturally urged a strong line against the dictators; Beaverbrook, friend of Hoare and a right wing capitalist in his own right, was an appeaser.

Sometime in 1937 Frank Owen paid an evening visit to Churchill at Chartwell, his home in Kent. He had been invited to interview the great man. Frank produced a long memo for Beaverbrook, explaining that the conversations had lasted from dinner at 8 until 2.30 am in Winston's bedchamber. The interview detailed his opposition to Mussolini, Hitler, Japan, Ramsay Mac-Donald, Stanley Baldwin and appeasers in general.

Having disposed of all that, Frank then put the boot in: 'By this time, which was near 2 o'clock, he (Churchill) waxed Napoleonic and having got off his shirt and trousers marched up and down in his pants and his vest, picking up busts of the great man and casting one eye at his great ancestor (the Duke of Marlborough) who looks down on him with both eyes from all angles.

'He declared he was strongly in favour of kings and against dictators, to whom he denied all the rights of military pomp, salutes etc . . .

'He then dragged out from his vast Napoleonic library 8 or 9 books of Napoleon's despatches which he read to us in execrable French vilely translated, with terrific energy, to demonstrate Napoleon's vast comprehension of detail. The most complete of those was a despatch 4½ pages long detailing the entry into Berlin after Jena, laying down the disposition and order of procession of forces into the conquered city. When he came within two lines of the end of this lengthy despatch, he discovered that it was not written by Napoleon but by Berthier, the Chief of Staff. So he read us two more despatches by the Master dealing with the Battle of Friedland.'

Frank concluded: 'I found him extraordinarily stimulating, high spirited, abounding in vigour and full of confidence, very encouraging and kindly.'

Beaverbrook sent the full text of the interview to Churchill, who was not amused. He wrote back: 'I return you Frank Owen's note of our very private and informal after-dinner conversation, which certainly gives a loose and sloppy impression of what I said, or did not say . . . It gives a much better picture of F.O. than it does of me.'

It must have been clear to Beaverbrook that sending this interview to Churchill with the implied threat to publish would infuriate the politician and throw a broad hint that his articles were no longer welcome at the *Standard*. It was not long before the newspaper dispensed with Churchill who took his by-line to the *Daily Telegraph*.

And, as for Frank Owen, he marched into 1938, year of Anschluss and Munich, very much heeding his master's voice, though occasionally allowed to lift his leg against the wrong tree.

6. STANDARD TRIUMPH

An editor of genius in the Fleet Street of
1939 – 41 when London was living through her
finest hours —

Michael Foot

PERCY CUDLIPP quit the editor's chair of the *Evening
Standard* early in 1938. Enough was enough under the
hectoring regime of general manager Mike Wardell and
the eldest of Bessie Cudlipp's three journalistic sons
moved to the Labour *Daily Herald* as editorial manager.

He had been an ideal choice for the *Standard* of the
early Thirties, described by Michael Foot as the 'house
journal of the exclusive London West End'. His
background had been that of a theatre critic, a writer of
urbane essays and a librettist feeding topical revues with
up-to-the-minute verses. In 1933 Cudlipp had buckled
down well to the task of producing a paper, but now his
editorial power was being purloined by a hard man.

New Zealand-born David Low had been allowed the
cartoonist's traditional freedom of political expression
ever since he joined the *Standard* from the *Star* in the
mid-1920s. The Nazis objected to his biting portrayals
of Hitler and Co. As a result, Low was summoned by
Wardell, over Cudlipp's head, to meet Foreign Sec-

retary Lord Halifax who put pressure on the cartoonist to be kinder to the Dictators.

At about the same time, November, 1937, Wardell was one of several Press owners and executives Halifax undertook to 'square' at the request of Sir Neville Henderson, who asked for British Press comment to be muzzled to help his appeasement work as British Ambassador in Berlin.

Cudlipp was replaced by Reg Thompson, a 'safe pair of hands' who had fought through the trenches with the Royal Fusiliers and was No. 2 under Christiansen at the *Daily Express*. It was he who had the task of terminating Churchill's contract with *Standard*, but in the August Thompson left 'on holiday' to be succeeded temporarily and then permanently by Frank Owen when it was announced that Thompson had been signed up by the *Daily Sketch*.

Editor Frank never had trouble with Wardell. They were well-matched, a couple of pirates. Frank, who sometimes claimed to be descended from Elizabethan sea dogs, was a freebooting Captain Henry Morgan to the William Kidd of the black eye-patched Wardell.

Mischievously the king of the pirates, Beaverbrook, set up squabbles between his buccaneer captains at Cherkley but the line between editorial and management on the *Standard* was now generally honoured. When war came both Frank Owen and Mike Wardell served on Mountbatten's SEAC staff, allied in the task of building troop morale.

On Friday, September 30, 1938 Neville Chamberlain signed the Munich agreement with Hitler that effectively stripped the Czechoslovak State of its defences. It was the culmination of appeasement. The *Standard*'s brand new editor sprang to action. He took a positive anti-Nazi line, breaking ranks with the 'softly, softly, there will be no war' views that Beaverbrook caused to be blazoned across the front pages of both his *Express* papers.

Frank wrote after the war: 'On October 3, 1938, a week after Munich, we began a series of articles on *Mein Kampf* which up to that time few people in England (including the Foreign Secretary, Lord Halifax) had ever read. They told of the 'grisly, gibbering horror of race hatred,' of Hitler's army, labour corps, anti-Jewish frenzy, contempt of France and his determination to wipe her out, his ambitions in Europe and threats to Russia, his attacks on religion and civil liberty.

'They ran for three weeks, after which appeared the personal story of Adolf Hitler, ending with the murder of his colleagues in the June massacre of 1934. I wrote the lot.'

It was a massive task, first interpreting the turgid prose of Hitler's personal testament to a British public who found the revelation of Hitler's megalomaniac aims disturbing, then detailing the Nazis' bloody road to power. This concentrated campaign of full-page feature articles lasted a month − from the first Monday of October to the last Saturday, the 29th. The final instalment was headed 'The Night of the Long Knives' and described how Hitler destroyed the power of the Brownshirts, the street soldiers who had hoisted him to authority over the Reich, by organising a putsch to butcher their leaders.

The article clearly portrays the Nazis as murderous

On pages following: **Frank slams Hitler**

Evening Standard, Saturday,

THE NIGHT OF LONG KNIVES

HITLER'S power rested on the
Street.

It is the most fearful (because
the least responsible) of all
Empires. The Roman brothers
Gracchi, Rienzi, our own Wat
Tyler, France's Danton and
Boulanger, Russia's Father Gapon
—or again our A. J. Cook—proved
the fickleness of the mob towards
its leader.

Hitler resolved to sell out—
before the mob-empire crucified
him.

* * *

STORM Troop Chief-of-Staff Ernst
Rohm, squat, pock-marked, battle-
scarred, brilliant "soldier with civilian
courage," had really only one idea in his
bullet-head.

It was as simple—and disastrous—as
that which filled the brain of the first
Frederick of Prussia. To go on adding
..rs. ....ring of 1934 Rohm had
...th of ...0,000 men,

and loot the capitalists. They were throw
only a few Jews.

In June 1933 three months after he
been confirmed in power as Chanc
Hitler announced " the National Revo
is at an end." The National-S
Storm Troops continued to cherish
of the Second and Socialist Revolt
The impending death o' Hi
loomed up Who would su
veteran President?

* * *

HITLER, of course, had
succeed. But for thi
carried the supreme comm
the loyalty of the Reichsy
The Reichswehr point
recognise the Storm Tro
ment increased and t
soldiers grew, the Reic
draw upon the mor
reserve formed by t
they resolutely ref
Brownshirts in u
join the Reichs
soldier and sub
traditional Prus
By the beg
speaking of " t
Six months b
Ernst Rohm
able servic
gratefully
fighter" B
describing
such tha
.. v ...

THE

The Story Behind "MEIN KAMPF"

They shot Von Schleicher down at breakfast. They shot his wife down too.

r
on
list
idea
nburg
d the

ecided to
ost. which
he needed

refused to
As rearma-
need for more
chr were glad to
less disciplined
torm Troops. But
to incorporate the
Every man must
as an individual
to all the rigours of
discipline.
g, of June Hitler was
thy Brownshirt clique.
he had written to "dear
hank him for "imperish-
and to describe him
"my friend and fellow
end of June he would be
as vile "Their conduct was
as impossible to invite them
or to cross the threshold of
staff." Rohm was a notorious
ut Hitler had known that

forgotten the days when these fine gentle-
men ruled from their easy chairs!"
But Hindenburg sent Von Papen a telegram of congratulation.
Toiling ceaselessly also was ex-
Reichswehr General Kurt von Schleicher.
who had also been dished by Hitler,

*   *   *

ROHM went off on furlough. He hoped to
relieve his liver of the afflictions
which his drunkenness imposed upon it
Before departing, in a general order to
the Storm Troops he scoffed at talk of dis-

for his viciousness, his cruelty or his crime.
Rohm was put into a car and driven back
to Munich. He was thrown into a cell, a
revolver was laid on the table. "No!" said
Rohm, who had killed many men and nev
feared to look on death, "If Adolf wants
shoot me, he can do it himself." After
hours he was led out and placed against
wall.

Several hundred made the same
walk. Karl Ernst, Hayn, Heydelree
Lasch Uhl—they were the heroes
Brownshirt army. All day, all n
Black Guard squads lined the
yards firing, firing. Ernst, dr
from the boat at Hamburg as l
on holiday with his young wif
been best man), fell believ

gangsters. There is none of the respectful pussyfooting that had most of the British press compulsorily referring to Herr Hitler, Doctor Goebbels, Field Marshal Goering and Signor Mussolini. Owen describes how Hitler, 'strangling the wolf that had suckled him', took a personal part in the violence, beating a Brownshirt senseless with repeated blows of his whip. The point is not whether that particular incident happened; rather it is the fact that such an action was attributed to a world leader in the pages of a Beaverbrook newspaper.

A decade later Beaverbrook commended the piece as 'a most brilliant, illuminating and savage article attacking Hitler and his associates' (this from a man who in June 1938 had told Frank to stop needling Ribbentrop). He added: 'Frank Owen had the freedom as editor of the *Evening Standard* to dissent from my support for the policy on Munich.' This was in a letter to the *Leader* magazine in August 1949.

A groundswell had emerged in the late 1930s of populist anti-fascist writing that focussed the feelings of ordinary British people already disquieted by the march of Mussolini and Hitler. They flocked to read a series of new publications.

It was Frank Owen's achievement to steer the previously pro-Establishment Evening Standard on to this groundswell. He swung hard a-port from a starboard tack.

The first writings to attract our attention are those circulated by the Left Book Club. This series of drab orange-covered softbacks appeared under the imprint of Victor Gollancz and the books were chosen by Harold Laski and John Strachey. They followed the Marxist line and fiercely supported the Republican cause in Spain.

The club was an instant success, attracting 60,000 subscribers who often banded together in local discussion groups. They were strong among schoolteachers and working class intelligentsia. In the South Wales Valleys, for instance, those who would in past years have gathered to argue the theology of profound sermons in chapel vestries now debated Marx, Lenin and the passions of international politics in miners' institutes and the cafes of Rabaiotti, Ricci and Lusardi.

In 1937 publisher Allen Lane founded Penguin Books, Britain's first real paperbacks at sixpence (2½p) a time. The lists of reprints were quickly supplemented by Penguin Specials, mainly originals which espoused the anti-fascist crusade. American reporter Ed Mowrer's *Germany Puts the Clock Back* appeared in December, 1937, to be quickly followed by G T Garratt on *Mussolini's Roman Empire*, French journalists Madame Tabouis' *Blackmail or War* and *Searchlight on Spain* by the maverick Tory Duchess of Atholl, a friend of Megan Lloyd George. All achieved massive sales.

A mass circulation weekly picture magazine, revolutionary in design, picture handling and news treatment, followed in October, 1938. This was *Picture Post*, selling at threepence and quickly paying its way on the news stands. Stefan Lorant, the first editor was a refugee from the Nazis and the line he took, with the full approval of proprietor Edward Hulton, was staunchly anti-appeasement.

Add to this Kingsley Martin's *New Statesman, Tribune* (soon to be edited by Nye Bevan), the clinical probing by A J Cummings of Nazi misdeeds in his *News Chronicle* Spotlight column, the angry rumblings of the

Daily Mirror's Cassandra . . . Frank Owen was in stimulating company.

This barrage, thunderous by the time of Munich, created a strong climate of opinion. As Angus Calder wrote in *The People's War*: 'For the first time the issues began to clarify for the 'men in the street', two-thirds of whom, Mass Observation found, felt that the Prime Minister should have defied the Fuhrer.'

Frank, meanwhile, had more than Hitler on his mind. He was busily pursuing a leggy American showgirl across Europe when circumstances allowed. She was Grace Stewart McGillivray, a Bostonian who had turned up in London as a member of the Grosvenor House midnight revue *Park Avenue to Park Lane*.

The company moved on to Paris, Vienna, Berlin and so on. Frank would turn up at these capitals, risking the vagaries of inter-war civil air services and sometimes arriving back late to face an angry Max Beaverbrook, who was the man who introduced Grace and Frank and fancied her himself. The editor and his lady were wed in February 1939 – a marriage which, improbably, lasted without rancour or children until Grace's death 29 years later.

When Beaverbrook moved Frank Owen to the *Standard*, he needed a new leader writer for the *Express* and set his mind on Geoffrey Cox, the group's New Zealand-born Paris correspondent, but was turned down flat by a man who held strong anti-appeasement views. Post-war, Cox became the father figure of British commercial TV news.

The great man then turned to a 25-year-old political journalist without national newspaper experience. Enter, left, Michael Foot, youngest of four illustrious

Grace

brothers from the West Country and the only avowed Socialist among them. His other passion: Plymouth Argyle FC.

Foot was invited to Cherkley, told to 'gut' that day's papers and, when Beaverbrook had read the synopsis, offered £9-a-week. This was riches. The young writer accepted on the spot and was sent to join Frank Owen for training on the *Standard*. He never did, in fact, take up the *Daily Express* job for which he was intended and remained as Frank's assistant and then successor on the evening paper.

Foot wrote in *Debts of Honour*: 'During those next months, indeed the next year or two, he gave me an intensive pressure-course introduction to the world, the flesh, the devil and his notion of Beaverbrook, not troubling always to draw too sharp a distinction between the last two on the list.

'He was himself a superlative journalist and editor . . . But the man was even more appealing than the journalist. His high spirits had a god-like quality. His physical capacity was such that he could drink all night everything and anything set before him and be hard at work at his desk, after a couple of Coca Colas, at seven o'clock next morning . . .

'Women fell for him in droves, at a glance; no one else I saw was ever in the same competition. Yet he did not treat the matter offensively but rather as if this triumphant promiscuity had been the natural lot of man (and woman) since Adam or soon after.'

In such manner did the young Harry look upon Falstaff, but Michael never forsook his picaresque hero.

That was one ally for Frank in the *Standard*'s anti-Fascist crusade. Another was already in place, the cartoonist Low whose wigging from Lord Halifax had hardly tamed his graphic invective. One drawing published in the middle of the *Mein Kampf* series was prophetic. It showed Hitler in Santa Claus rig throwing a succession of small boys into his sack. Little Master Austria was already in, Czechoslovakia on his way and Poland, Hungary, Yugoslavia, Romania, Bulgaria, Greece and Turkey queuing up ready. As it turned out only Turkey missed the jackboot. The cartoon was captioned: Europe can look forward to a Christmas of peace — Hitler.

And almost a year later just after the outbreak of war when Germany and Russia signed a shock pact, Low had Hitler and Stalin greeting each other over the prostrate body of Poland. Says Hitler: 'The scum of the earth, I believe.' Replies Stalin: 'The bloody assassin of the workers, I presume'.

With Poland quickly dismembered, the dreaded blitz on the Western Front just did not happen — that winter. But the *Standard* did not sleep. Foot wrote: 'In the months of the phoney war, while Beaverbrook himself was still sulking in his appeaser's tent, Frank Owen started to fashion the paper into what it truly became, a combined sword and shield for the people of London.'

And Geoffrey Cox recalls a mid-March, 1940 dinner at Stornoway House, a month or two before Hitler unleashed his Panzers in the West. Among Beaverbrook's other guests were *Daily Express* editor Christiansen, Frank Owen and Grace. At that time US Assistant Secretary of State Sumner Welles was on a peace mission to Europe. Beaverbrook took this up, asking each guest in turn: 'Are you for peace?' But when he came to Owen and Cox, he said: 'I'm not going to ask you. I know your views. You are both for war.' Lord Gnome was beginning to see the light.

7. CATO'S CURSE

We have sustained a defeat without a war —
Churchill (on Munich)

THREE angry young men talked on the roof of the *Evening Standard* building in Shoe Lane EC4. It was a pleasant place to loiter on a May evening in 1940, to clear one's nostrils of the reek of hot printing metal, to unwind in the dead period between seeing the last edition to bed and opening time at the Two Brewers.

Southward lay the glass *Express* building and the view across Fleet Steet to where the Thames flowed, east beyond the drab canyon of Farringdon Street stood St Paul's, northward in Holborn was Gamages, department store of the lower middle classes. But the minds of the trio were focussed far from the London skyline.

Standard editor Frank Owen, assistant Michael Foot and their frequent boozing mate, Peter Howard of the *Sunday Express*, were discussing Dunkirk, where at that moment a large section of the British Expeditionary Force was being snatched from the jaws of the German Panzer armies.

The three journalists were agreed. They would write an instant pamphlet explaining how this defeat of the Allies was the direct result of appeasement and pillorying those politicians they deemed responsible for that disastrous policy. The aim was to drive such culprits as Neville Chamberlain, Lord Halifax and Sir John Simon out of the new Churchill coalition Cabinet.

The rooftop conference was on Friday, May 31 and by the following Tuesday the 30,000-word diatribe had been completed. Foot devised the title, *Guilty Men*, from an incident in the French Revolution and the three authors cloaked themselves under the by-line 'Cato', from Cato the Younger who had made a famous speech denouncing Julius Caesar.

They split the work between them, Foot taking the first chapter, which was emotive, second-hand reportage of the scenes on the Dunkirk beaches, and Owen writing a sharp critique of blitzkrieg and why the Allies so woefully failed to counter such tactics. All three authors shared the rest of the chapters which flayed the MacDonald, Baldwin and Chamberlain Governments from 1929 up to Munich and Dunkirk.

The most valid arguments are in Frank Owen's Blitzkrieg chapter. He starts with the point that Munich took four Czech armoured divisions (compared with Germany's five at the time) out of the game without a shot fired. He then analyses tactics used by the Germans in the West – coordination of tanks, motorised infantry, mobile artillery and planes, plus planned infiltration – and points out that they were methods perfected in World War I and used against the Republicans in the Spanish Civil War. Frank suggests that what the Allies needed was defence in depth (zones instead of static lines) and an adequate mobile reserve.

Parts of the original manuscript (written by Howard) were deemed libellous and sub-edited accordingly.

*Frank Owen's GUILTY MEN collaborators — Michael Foot and
Peter Howard*

Howard was an Old Millhillian rugby forward who went on to captain England and Oxford University. He was discovered by Beaverbrook when he spoke up at an Empire Crusade meeting and quickly taken on as a trainee political writer. He was a man of moods and more intemperate in his views than the other two writers. He finished up as a religious leader with Moral Rearmament.

An agent was hired. He made an immediate deal with publisher Victor Gollancz and, as Foot wrote later, did in fact run away with part of the royalties.

The two big national wholesalers, Smiths and Wymans, refused to handle the book, which effectively boosted sales. Eighteen impressions were printed in the first two months and the yellow-dustcovered hardback, which sold at 2s 6d (12½p), ran to a total of 250,000 copies before the 1945 General Election.

It had a tremendous impact. I remember, as a politically-aware sixth-former, trawling the Cardiff bookshops for a copy and reading it completely before the old Great Western 'rattler' reached my Valleys home. It was a bootlegged book. Lord Elton, the historian, recalled seeing it sold on the pavement at Whitehall 'as though it were pornography'. Foot tells how the trio made arrangements to sell *Guilty Men* from barrows around Ludgate Circus and Charing Cross.

This volume of 120 or so pages had two flaws, one of which was to make Beaverbrook happy and the other to give tremendous aid to the Labour Party. Nowhere in the book was there any reference to his lordship's steady and often vociferous support for appeasement, his trumpeting that there would be 'no war this year – or next'. All the other players are savaged, including such minor figures as Sir Thomas Inskip ('Caligula's horse' as defence coordinator) and Captain David Margesson, whose offence was doing his job efficiently as Chief Government Whip.

If the three authors took the name Cato to fool their employer, they certainly did nothing to implicate him among the guilty in the text. When he did find out, he had no beef.

The other flaw was the ruthless lack of balance in the case presented. It was total political propaganda. Press Association political reporter A H Booth called *Guilty Men* 'a slender but potent volume which for five years had been almost bursting its yellow dust-jacket with moral indignation'.

Labour's 1945 landslide election was won on two fronts, that of Munich and that of Jarrow. In the first instance *Guilty Men* was an obvious factor with 250,000 copies sold, many of them in lending libraries up and down the land. The powerful social concience of *Picture Post*, the most important journalistic voice of the period, did perhaps a more legitimate job of hammering the Jarrow nail into the Conservatives whose pre-war social and economic record had been deplorable.

But all that was in the future and we return to Frank Owen preparing to grapple with a war that had ceased to be phoney. He had schooled himself well, cultivating a panel of military gurus with unorthodox views.

The most significant of these was John 'Boney' Fuller. In his Cambridge tripos Frank had made a special study of the American Civil War. Fuller, at one stage chief instructor at the Imperial Staff College and colleague of Bernard Montgomery, published in 1923 a book that was of particular interest to Frank Owen. It was called *Grant and Lee: A Study in Personality and Generalship*. Much acclaimed by American historians, it became an essential part of the Cambridge student's reading. In 1929 Fuller produced a more detailed study of Grant. General Fuller and the young MP were on a wavelength.

Fuller saw the American conflict as the first modern war with its trenches, barbed wire, mortars, grenades, machine guns and dum-dum bullets. In addition to such technology, it was the first clash of industrial populations, much more 'total' in its nature than, say, either the Crimean or Boer Wars. Fuller wrote many years later: 'Had the nations of Europe studied the lessons of the Civil War and taken them to heart, they would not in 1914 – 18 have perpetrated the enormous tactical blunders of which that war bears record.'

Fuller's second big theme was his total belief in the combination of tanks and close support aircraft to drive through static troops, leaving open flanks and overrunning territory to be mopped up at leisure. While the Allies failed to grasp the idea, it was the very means by which Hitler won his 1940 triumph in the West. His Panzer generals, like Guderian and Rommel, were disciples of Fuller, who quit his British Army career as a 55-year-old major general because he could not convince the Salisbury Plain strategists.

Thirdly, Fuller strongly disapproved of the 'indirect approach' strategy which dissipated military effort on such ventures as Gallipoli in World War I and the Italian campaign of World War II. This put him very much into the vanguard of those who demanded 'Second Front now' when Russia was invaded by Hitler, rather than put resources into extending Mediterranean operations to penetrate the 'soft belly of the Axis', in Churchill's phrase.

Both the belief in armour and the need for an early cross-Channel invasion, were strong in Owen's mind. Though Fuller, in his frustration, had been a black-shirted follower of Sir Oswald Mosley, Frank employed him to write articles for the *Standard*, notably four in early January 1942 which roused great controversy. In answer to critics Frank wrote: 'I have long thought General Fuller should have a post in the Government . . . I do not agree with the general's politics but have a great respect for his military strategy.'

Earlier there had been an association with Basil Liddell Hart, another pro-tank propagandist, but he fell out of favour with the *Standard* because of his belief in 'indirect approach' strategy.

Frank Owen also admired Archibald Wavell, whose service with Allenby against the Turks in World War I had made him the apostle of mobility and manoeuvre. As Middle East commander-in-chief he worked on a shoestring yet managed to capture both Abyssinia and most of Libya from the Italians in simultaneous campaigns.

It was through Wavell that Owen was able to cultivate possibly the most original military thinker of this century. Michael Foot recalls how a young major of artillery called Orde Wingate drank Owen under the table in 1938 at the editor's Lincoln's Inn flat.

The oddball major was a thinker before his time. As a pre-war staff officer in Palestine he had perfected guerilla tactics that gave the Jews, including youthful Moshe Dayan, many victories over the Arabs. In 1940 Wavell asked for Wingate and despatched him over the

Abyssinian frontier in command of the tiny Gideon Force which put whole Italian divisions on the wrong foot.

An even more impressive example of Wingate's infiltration tactics came after Wavell, now moved to India, recruited him again. The organisation of the Chindits for undercover operations in the Burmese jungles frustrated the Japanese and laid the foundations for Slim's final victory. General Wingate, much studied in the second half of this century by both political terrorists and forces like the SAS, was killed in a Burmese air crash not long after Frank Owen arrived in the area to run the command Forces newspaper.

This series of military contacts certainly furnished Frank's mind and what he learned from the generals helped make him such a thorn in the side of Churchill and the cautious British high command.

8. LOVE IN THE BLITZ

The bewilderingly beautiful Anna —
Sefton Delmer

A slow boat and an old flame led Anna Maclaren into Frank Owen's life. The affair they began in 1940 was to last, including intervals, 20 years.

Anna, daughter of popular novelist Mark Channing, had left her husband pre-war to stride the catwalk for Paris dress designer Elsa Schiaparelli in the Place Vendôme. During the phoney war Paris retained its social glitter. Donald Maclean, later unmasked as fellow-spy of Burgess and Philby, frequently escaped his British Embassy duties to drink the night clubs dry. Suddenly, however, the real war arrived as the Panzers exploded through Northern France. The Government fled Paris for Bordeaux, the emergency capital.

The British community, among them Anna Maclaren, joined the exodus. In Bordeaux she bumped into Maclean who gave her one of the scarce tickets to join SS Madura, the last ship for England. It was a frightening, uncomfortable voyage for the assorted foreign correspondents, diplomats and stray Service people, of whom Anna was one from her membership of the Section Sanitaire Automobile, a volunteer military ambulance unit.

Madura stole down the Gironde Estuary to the Bay of Biscay, stood out into the Atlantic to round Ushant and enter the mouth of the English Channel. Those aboard the tardy old rust-bucket were very conscious that the U-boat fleet was prowling waters suddenly denuded of British destroyer cover. When the 7,000-ton Madura eventually tied up at Falmouth crammed to the gunnels with almost 2,000 passengers she had survived several near misses from Luftwaffe bombs.

In London Anna met an old friend, Zöe Farmer, a *Daily Express* feature writer. 'I'm looking for a job,' said Anna. Zöe, who had been Frank Owen's mistress in the mid-1930s and was then married to Sydney Bernstein (of later Granada TV fame), gave Anna an introduction to the *Standard* editor. Looking back more than 50 years later, Anna said: 'After our chat Zöe gave me a quizzical look and said: "I know what will happen." And it did!'

'I joined the paper on space, writing paragraphs on a freelance basis, taking to heart Frank's advice: "Write what you know about." We were soon very close. At the beginning of the Blitz on London in August 1940, I had a beautiful flat in Gray's Inn Road. Mike Foot used to say that the bombing went unheeded by Frank and me at this time. One evening as we walked back to the flat with bombs and debris raining all round, Frank put his hands – very beautiful and expressive ones – over my brow "to protect your pretty head" as he said.

'I stayed with Frank and the *Standard* until he was called up to the Army in the spring of 1942. He and Mike Foot made a wonderful editorial pair. There

Anna

cannot have ever been anything like it in Fleet Street: The fire and white hot sincerity and enthusiasm that those two generated.

'Michael's rapier wit and Frank's ebullient forcefulness combined to make an irresistible force. They even swept Beaverbrook off his feet. It is a wonder Michael's delicate constitution survived the titanic bouts of alcoholic consumption. I used to sit silent and in awe listening to the cut and thrust of their polemics in the Two Brewers saloon bar without really understanding what the arguments were all about. Mike had – has – more depth of mind and character in a frailer body whereas Frank was the epitome of masculine charisma, with force, looks, physique, the lot.'

From Anna we get a picture of Frank's habits and tastes. He drank whisky and champagne and 'also liked Pouilly Fumé which we always had when lunching at L'Escargot'. If he was ordering a round of drinks and somebody asked for a single Scotch, his rejoinder was: 'Don't make a fool of your mouth. Have a double.'

'He was a very small eater, as most heavy drinkers are,' said Anna, 'but he liked simple things like grilled sole. Frank was not a habitual smoker but usually accepted a cigarette if offered and smoked it very amateurishly. That was the conventional politeness of the time. He sang in a musical voice, usually *Sospan Fach*, the Welsh rugby ditty. He could be very sentimental and grieved over a poodle called Joey which died when he and Grace were in Westminster Mansions.'

Frank, apparently, had no conventional hobbies, few outside interests like theatre, arts and cinema. Anna said: 'He was always totally concentrated on his work. History and politics were his interests almost to the exclusion of everything else.'

This exclusion never applied to women. The first name to crop up is that of Mary Edwards, a friend of his sister in Hereford and daughter of a local businessman. This was a conventional family-approved romance and came to nothing. Mary went on to marry twice. First she was Mrs Brown and then Mrs Blashford-Snell, step-mother of a famous explorer.

Frank's other known youthful amour was picaresque. A few years after the war a 17-year-old girl called Iris travelled to London in search of her father. Anna recalls she was a very beautiful girl, daughter of a Hereford barmaid. Frank eventually paid her fare to America where she wanted to join the Scientology cult. Ten years later she rang Anna to say 'she was married with a brood of children and living as a New Age person'.

In Fleet Street, as we have seen, there had been the tragic Patsy who died of an overdose and journalist Zöe Farmer who left him to marry Bernstein in 1936. This marriage did not survive the War and Zöe eventually died by her own hand.

One powerful rumour among journalists was that Frank Owen had been the lover of the outrageous Black Venus of Paris nightlife, Josephine Baker, the Banana Dance girl. He did not try very hard to discourage this reputation but the truth revealed a much more humble conquest. He was at one time during the Thirties frequently in the company of Nina Mae McKinney, a black dancer at Frisco's club. Her catchword was: 'Why don't you and me make bunjee!' – whatever that was.

Anna Phillips summed up: 'Frank's attraction for women was legendary and I, for one, found him irresistible. Many were smitten but few were laid – at least while I was about.'

9. TROOPER

Through mud, through blood to the green fields
beyond —

Tank Corps motto

DISTRUST of Winston Churchill's war strategy created
the 1941-2 alliance of Nye Bevan and Frank Owen. Ten
or more years previously they had been flatmates in the
Cromwell Road area, a couple of radicals prepared to
argue the night through, each cutting his polemic teeth
on the other's intellect.

Now they had a common cause: The relief of
embattled Russia by launching the earliest possible
Allied invasion across the Channel. Bevan edited
Tribune and called upon the fiery writing talents of
Owen, Michael Foot and Claud Cockburn. From the
left wing *Tribune*'s editorial offices in the Strand they
used the nearby Savoy as their 'pub'. Contemporary
reporter Jean Nicol wrote: 'Aneurin Bevan brought his
diatribes against Mr Churchill wet from the printing
press into the comfort of the American Bar.'

The Second Front agitation made Frank enemies in
the Cabinet. Bevan was recognised as incorrigible and,
as an MP, untouchable; neither Foot nor Cockburn had
the charisma and presence of the *Standard* editor who

was reckoned a dangerous loose cannon. His sudden call-up into the Army early in 1942 was seen by many as a calculated pounce by the authorities, though it was not quite as simple as that.

In November 1938 the Civil Service had prepared a schedule of reserved occupations. In the following year this supplemented the National Service (Armed Forces) Act under which all men from 18 to 41 were liable for conscription. Different reservation ages applied according to the job. Miners, for instance, were totally reserved; professional footballers not at all. From November 1939 employers could seek deferment of key workers below reservation age. Frank Owen as the 34-year-old editor of a substantial evening paper, would clearly have had no trouble on any account in staying in Civvy Street.

But the manpower shortage by July 1941 not only extended the call-up to a top age of 51 but also caused the ending of block reservations, putting the onus on employers to apply to district manpower boards for individual deferments − each on its own merits.

In newspapers the policy was that any editor, sub-editor or responsible executive over 30 was deferred for periods of three to six months when further applications could be made. Clearly somebody in the Beaverbrook organisation overlooked this. It could have been Frank himself. He was always neglectful of administrative paper work.

Hannen Swaffer recounted the call-up story: On Wednesday, March 25, 1942, Frank was the personal guest of General Sir Bernard Paget, formidable commander of home forces, watching manoeuvres in the North. He had originally met the gruff general a fortnight previously. Paget was impressed by Frank's opinions on German strategy and said: 'Your views would make an admirable Army manual.'

On Thursday, March 26, he reported at a Royal Armoured Corps depot where he became 'Trooper Owen, H. F.'

On Friday, March 27, Frank was given three weeks leave to clear up his desk at the *Standard* – a privilege vouchsafed few conscripts.

On Sunday, March 29, he had been due to chair a Second Front Now rally at Trafalgar Square. As a serving soldier he was not allowed to take any active part and watched silently as Cassandra, the Daily Mail columnist, John Gordon and Eric Baume addressed the throng.

The inference of a draconian swoop by Labour and National Service Minister Ernest Bevin was quickly taken up, not least by 'Lord Haw Haw', William Joyce, the Nazis' English language propagandist on Radio Hamburg and Bremen. Swaffer said this was a silly invention: 'Frank lost his deferment papers, went in, then refused to come out.'

Beaverbrook, now out of the War Cabinet and supporting the Second Front agitation, was still convinced he could persuade his former colleagues to release Frank but was not amused when his editor in khaki said publicly: 'I'm with a fine lot of chaps and I'm going to see it through.'

Before he left, Fleet Street's finest gave Frank a farewell dinner. Swaffer, Percy Cudlipp, Arthur Christiansen and the *News Chronicle*'s A J Cummings spoke, as did Michael Foot who took over the *Standard*.

Frank Owen was an unusual rookie trooper – much

older than most at 37, very tall at 6 ft 2 in for a corps that had to pack troops into tiny compartments, lacking mechanical aptitude despite the sophistication of his intellect. Two things were not to his liking – heavy boots and hard, lumpy beds composed of three square 'biscuits' which added to the discomfort. But he relished the physical challenge. His leisure interests had always been strenuous: Rugby, rowing and boxing.

Recruits did an initial seven weeks in the Salisbury Plain area. Apart from the usual square bashing, route marches and gymnastics, they learned the basics of the tank trades – driving, gunnery, and wireless – and were then allocated to the specialisations they would take up in a combat regiment. The young troopers were often industrial apprentices, transport drivers and bright lads straight from secondary school. They were an eye-opener for Frank. He told fellow-journalist Tom Driberg: 'What surprised me was that the considerable natural intelligence of my fellow-troopers was so often combined with an appalling political and general ignorance. But their astonishing technical facility constantly shamed my clumsy fingers.'

The link with Nye Bevan remained. The Welsh MP venerated a Leveller of the Civil War era, Colonel Thomas Rainsborough, who had faced down the mighty Cromwell in bitter political argument. Therefore when Bevan fired new broadsides at Churchill in *Tribune* he chose the by-line Thomas Rainsboro' to hide the identity of the author, who was Frank Owen, risking court martial, if not quite treason charges, if he had been caught.

There were three articles – on May 1, 8 and 15. The first two detailed military 'blunders' by Churchill in

Norway, Greece, North Africa and Malaya. The last one condemned Government sloth over aid to Russia and delaying the Second Front until the Allies could build up overwhelming strength. Frank concluded: 'If we could go on piling up arms until 1943 and then crack Hitler on the snout, it would be admirable. But what is Hitler going to be engaged in until 1943? War is not an addition sum but an equation in time. Have we time to afford Churchill's strategy?'

The Rainsboro' attacks infuriated the war leaders and military intelligence began closing in. Beaverbrook got wind of this and asked Michael Foot: 'When's the next article due from Frank?' On being told 'This week', Beaverbrook said 'You'd better stop it — tonight.'

Foot drove to Andover, 'scoured the pubs, found Frank, took the copy off him, started to race back to London, crashed the car on the humped bridge on the London road outside Andover, and was taken off for repairs to the nearest Army camp who put me on the road next morning.' If the War Office had known whom they were helping . . .

That was the end of Rainsboro' and Frank duly moved north to Catterick where he joined an operational tank regiment. Anna had meanwhile married a well-heeled character called Rodney Phillips who turned up in the same regiment as Frank. When Rodney rang her, he often put Frank on the telephone to talk to her in London.

While Frank was a trooper several approaches came from people who wanted him to stand in Parliamentary by-elections, notably for the University of Wales seat late in 1942 and Peterborough less than a year later. This would have meant fighting as a radical independent. Because of the Coalition, the major parties were observing an electoral truce.

Frank declined to get involved. He was taking the Army seriously and keen to become an officer. His arrival at Blackdown Camp for a course is recalled by Tony Pyatt, now a retired Ipswich newspaper editor.

'It was in 1943,' Pyatt said. 'I was an instructor at a pre-OCTU course and Frank Owen was in one of my classes. He found it tough going to master the technicalities of tank wireless. Most of his classmates were in the 18 to 20 bracket. He was well into his 30s. But he worked very hard and passed, allowing him to go on to Sandhurst for officer training. He would have made a good tank officer, but it was not to be.'

10. PASSAGE TO INDIA

Ship me somewheres east of Suez
Where the best is like the worst,
Where there aren't no Ten Commandments
And a man can raise a thirst
                    Kipling's Mandalay

LOUIS Mountbatten had a problem. At the Anglo-American Quebec Conference in August, 1943, Churchill offered him the biggest challenge of his youthful Service career. The man who had started the war commanding a flotilla of destroyers and was then rocketed into the control of Combined Operations became, at the stroke of the Churchillian pen, the supreme commander of a theatre of operations – South East Asia. He was 43.

Lord Louis, a minor Royal, had never lacked confidence. He was sure he could handle the logistics and battle problems of his new command. And cope with the cohort of officers in SEAC whose seniority in all three services he had leapfrogged.

But one thing worried him: Morale. The Japanese had made a headlong drive into Burma. Then, when they were held on the Indian border, Allied attempts to reconquer the Arakan ended in defeat in May,

81

1943, after six months fighting, 2,500 battle casualties and an even longer malaria roll. The troops, a long way from home, felt themselves dispirited, a forgotten army.

They needed, Dickie Mountbatten decided, their own bright, optimistic newspaper like the *Union Jack* which boosted morale on the Italian Front under the editorship of the *Daily Mirror's* Hugh Cudlipp.

'Where do I find an editor,' Mountbatten asked his staff. 'The man you need is Frank Owen,' said Brigadier Mike Wardell, a friend of Lord Louis from Prince of Wales's Set days and later a Beaverbrook colleague of Frank's.

Mountbatten wrote in May 1946: 'If we were to fight a campaign of indefinite duration, thousands of miles away, we should all need to feel that we were still in touch, not only with what was happening in the world at large but also with what was going on at home.

'It would have to be edited as fairly and impartially as possible and it would have to be our own paper in which we could air our views. The man to solve our problem was Frank Owen. When I managed to trace him, he had just blossomed from a trooper RAC to a fully-fledged cadet and was with difficulty persuaded to abandon his ambition to be a second lieutenant in a tank.'

But Frank was easier to persuade than War Minister James Grigg, who involved Churchill in the dispute, saying that the journalist was thinking of standing as an anti-Government Parliamentary candidate. Churchill gave the appointment a thumbs down but Mountbatten stuck to his guns insisting that if Churchill had the confidence to make him a supreme commander, he must also have the belief to let him choose his own staff. 'I made an absolute issue of it and won,' he told his biographer, Philip Ziegler.

Frank Owen was commissioned second lieutenant on December 20, 1943, and in less than a fortnight was on his way to the Far East. The Admiralty were sending the 1st Battle Squadron to face the Japanese. The battleships Queen Elizabeth and Valiant plus the battlecruiser Renown left Scapa Flow on December 30 and were joined by the carriers Illustrious and Unicorn out of the Clyde. Frank took passage in Renown.

But in early January he was put ashore at Gibraltar and must have been flown on to India from there because the first copy of the newspaper, *SEAC*, was published in Calcutta on January 10. The battle squadron did not make landfall at Colombo until January 30 so they must have spent some weeks of seatime working up the Queen Elizabeth, recently recommissioned after a long refit, and training the carrier air squadrons in the unfamiliar methods of fighting the Japanese.

Frank, while ashore at Gibraltar, met Hugh Cudlipp's brother, Reginald, another Fleet Street journalist. He was producing the Rock's Forces newssheet.

Reginald, who was to become a post-war editor of the *News of the World*, told me: 'Frank took a lot of interest in my publications. He must have been impressed and asked if I could join him on *SEAC*. I suggested he put in an official request through Gibraltar Garrison and within three months I was on my way to Calcutta.'

SEAC was an outstanding success from the first issue. Air Chief Marshal Sir Philip Joubert, Mountbatten's deputy chief of staff for information, wrote: 'It is hard to say what the troops appreciated most: Owen's pungent leading articles that frequently got him – and me – into trouble with the War Office, the sports news or the Jane cartoon.'

Quoting Joubert, Ziegler's life of Mountbatten adds: 'Owen's indiscretions caused frequent turmoil in Whitehall.' One of these indiscretions is recalled by Frank's pre-war Fleet Street friend, Hugh Cudlipp, editor of the *Sunday Pictorial* until his call-up in 1940.

'Before I was seconded to edit and publish Army newspapers in the Central Mediterranean,' Hugh told me, 'I had the advantage of serving two years as an officer, an infantry platoon commander at El Alamein and then observer with the Desert Rats until we reached Tripoli. I was familiar with military pride and prejudice. I knew that the average commander from the rank of brigadier upwards feared the whiff of printer's ink more than the smell of the enemy's gunpowder.

'Journalists, even official journalists in uniform, even former editors, were regarded with lively suspicion by some generals. The ritual patriotic view in the officers' mess was that the establishment was always right and that to question the wisdom of authority was not a democratic right but subversive.

'Frank was commissioned only a month before he edited the first issue of *SEAC*. Even with the ironclad protection of Mountbatten, manifestly susceptible like Montgomery to published adulation in his own command newspaper, it was inevitable Frank would put a foot wrong now and then in the dangerous minefield of official journalism. I certainly did. Even when, in the judgment of any rational, impartial person, we were right, we were still tried *in absentia* with no appeal.

Generals were uniformly more scared of Cabinet disapproval than were former Fleet Street editors in uniform.'

Hugh Cudlipp went on to recall that on the day before he joined the Army at the end of 1940, he had a farewell drink at El Vino's with Frank Owen and Bill Connor, who was Cassandra, the *Daily Mirror* columnist.

'The next I heard from Frank,' said Hugh, 'was when Captain Owen was editor of *SEAC* and I was producing the third in a chain of daily *Union Jacks* in Naples. Subject: The bleakly low pay of the British soldiery in comparison with their US Army comrades in arms. Frank's questions, cabled unclassified, were: One, What was my attitude? Two, Should we run a joint campaign, he in *SEAC* and I in the *CMF* newspapers?

'The approach and proposal were not merely "indiscretions", they were potentially explosive. Nothing would have diverted Winston Churchill's attention from the conduct of the war more than a collaboration (conspiracy, in Churchillian language) by official Services newspapers to question Whitehall or Westminster policies. I had already received a jumbo rocket from the Cabinet via a reluctant General Sir Brian Robertson, Alexander's right-hand man (who said privately that he agreed with me), for printing letters from soldiers complaining about the disparity in pay with the Yanks.

'It was always difficult to persuade generals or Cabinet Ministers during wartime that grievances in the Services are not removed by suppression and that it was a proper function of newspapers, official or otherwise, to provide a safety-valve by presenting where possible both sides. I replied to Frank through the most secret channel available to me.

'The next Frank Owen-Hugh Cudlipp wartime contact involved not only Frank but Bill Connor (then serving as a Royal Artillery officer in the UK) and the enlightened General Sir Ronald Adam, Adjutant-General of the whole British Army. Adam, who really did understand the creditability factor in official newspapers, was wisely selected as Chairman of the world-wide British Council after the war. Early in 1944, on an official tour of the Mediterranean operation, General Adam entertained me to a splendid dinner, discussed my problems, then raised a problem of his own. Frank Owen, with Mountbatten's approval, had applied to have Lieut. William Connor transferred from the Royal Artillery to the Services newspaper *SEAC* to serve as a journalist.

'The Secretary of State for War, Sir James Grigg, was not at all happy about the idea; he had already unsuccessfully opposed the appointment of Owen. Bill Connor, appearing famously in the *Daily Mirror* up to the moment of his call-up as the radical daily columnist Cassandra, had an anti-Nazi record as a writer as impeccable as Churchill's as a political orator. He had, however, clashed with Prime Minister Churchill on several notorious occasions, criticising the inadequacy of the initial wartime Cabinet and Churchill's retention in power of the failed Municheers. Churchill had described him in a letter to Cecil King as "dominated by malevolence".

'Moreover, Cassandra's name was poison to the brasshats whose military idiosyncrasies he had persistently lampooned; ordering coalheaps in barracks to be whitewashed, obsessive button-polishing, church parades, saluting drill, etc. The notion of transferring Cassandra to Services newspapers, even as Lieut. William Connor, was lunatic, even if he were chained to a desk, blindfolded, with his writing arm amputated and his typewriter sledge-hammered.

'When the genial General Adam suggested a brandy I sensed what was coming. The request from Captain Owen could be deftly refused if Lieut. Colonel Cudlipp, Commanding Officer of the British Army Newspaper Unit in Central Mediterranean had already requested Lieut. Connor's services. The feeling back home, said Adam vaguely, was that as an old colleague I could "control" Cassandra more effectively than Frank. The trouble was that you can't say No to the Adjutant-General of the whole blooming British Army.'

What concerned Hugh Cudlipp, already battling with several generals in the field, Whitehall and vigilant members of the Cabinet to preserve some semblance of freedom for the official newspapers was that the arrival of Cassandra would lead to ultra right-wing MPs back home denouncing *Union Jack* as 'the *Daily Mirror* in khaki'. The sequel was described by Cudlipp in his book *Publish and Be Damned.*

He tells how Henry Longhurst, the golfing MP, asked the War Minister 'whether it was not extraordinary that Cassandra, whose writing helped to get the *Mirror* warned, should now be writing the same sort of thing in an Army paper.' War Minister Grigg, in reply, agreed with Labour's Fred Bellenger that articles by Cassandra and Frank Owen were helping boost troop morale.

The *Mirror* made a biting attack on Longhurst. 'In Italy,' Cudlipp wrote, 'Cassandra read this defence of his reputation. Then continued with the task upon which that day he was engaged – the writing of a waspish, vituperative, subversive article warning the troops of the dangers of excessive drinking or, as he called it, Demon Rum.'

Enter Jane

11. BURMA STAR

'Our own newspaper... *SEAC*... was
edited by Frank Owen... I had pulled him
out as a second lieutenant to tackle this
job. I gave him a completely free hand. And
he did it brilliantly.'

Earl Mountbatten (1968)

IF Frank Owen failed to land Cassandra, he certainly managed to net a more exotic bird from the *Daily Mirror*. This was Jane, the cartoon cutie who often found herself stripped to bra and pants at the end of a daily episode.

She was already appearing in *Union Jack* and the Submarine Service's paper. Now the third issue of *SEAC* proclaimed: 'Jane, the Strip Queen, arrived in Calcutta by air from London this morning. Interviewed by *SEAC*, she said: "Sorry boys, I'm too tired to take my clothes off now but I'll be with you in *SEAC* tomorrow and every day onwards".' She kept her word, constantly sacrificing modesty in the cause of military morale.

Controversy was never far away from Frank. *SEAC*'s last issue two years later recalled: 'When the paper was born . . . little-known Lieut. General William Slim was commanding a force charged with keeping the Japs out of India. That force was already the biggest of the British Imperial armies, but it was unnamed. The words "Fourteenth Army" were top secret.

'There was a feeling among the men that there, on the borders of Burma, they were unheeded, unsung, forgotten by the people at home.'

Frank cabled Churchill asking for a message of cheer for the 14th Army. It arrived in time for the second issue, in which it was published. 'The censors were apoplectic. Owen went strangely bland. Could we censor the Prime Minister? he asked. Correspondents cabled the story all over the world. Fourteenth Army was on the map.'

There was the case of the phantom brigadier. *SEAC* was hardly a dozen issues old when one of Frank's Tory enemies asked a Commons question about his remarkable promotion to brigadier. Grigg replied: 'I am informed he is still a second lieutenant.'

Tom Driberg wrote soon afterwards: 'Owen, with a couple of assistants, took the parcels (of *SEAC*) down to the airfield to speed them on their way to the troops. But the plane was full; the pilot would carry nothing more. Owen stamped and raved: It was the Commander-in-Chief's personal orders that the paper should be rushed to the front . . . there was no badge of rank on his uniform.

'One of his assistants joined in the argument, referring to him as "Brigadier Owen". The effect was instantaneous: it was a simple matter to off-load two colonels who stood by, purple with rage but mute with discipline, while bundles of *SEAC* were piled into the seats they had occupied!'

Soon, however, *SEAC* was allocated its own plane. Every morning it was loaded up at Calcutta with a ton of newsprint, 30,000 copies. They arrived at 14th Army head-quarters to be off-loaded and split into consignments which went on by road or air to every unit that could be reached, including those behind enemy lines. Journalists involved in the birth of the paper included Ian Coster, a New Zealander and old *Standard* colleague of Frank's, Len Jackson from the *Daily Mirror* and *Daily Express* man Tom Wilcox who had been in tanks with Frank. *SEAC* started as a daily but quickly added a Sunday edition. There were 852 issues in its 867-day life.

A big staff was needed. Conscripted reporters and sub-editors were combed out of their regiments, ships and air squadrons. And soon, into this newsy hive, arrived Reg Cudlipp, who recalled: 'I got there in the middle of the monsoon which makes wrecks of strong men. Frank had acquired printing and office facilities at *The Statesman* newspaper and staff living accommodation at the nearby Lake Paint House, recently vacated by a paint firm.'

Frank had few inhibitions, said Cudlipp. 'He was given to cooling off in the monsoon by going naked on to the balcony of the Lake Paint house in his leisure time and showering in the teeming rain. It gave nearby Indian house-holders a chance to appreciate Frank's splendid manhood.

'I still remember him giving birth to telling phrases of a leading article while standing topless in his office on a humid night with the fans battling valiantly. Suddenly their swirling action would catch up a sheaf of papers on which he was working and send them to all corners of the room with Frank dancing with rage and using his extensive vocabulary of swear words.'

Frank's editorials were fearless and forthright under the title 'Good Morning'. They gave the man at the sharp end a feeling that somebody up there on the staff was thinking of him and sometimes caused a general to choke on his breakfast kedgeree.

The four-page, smaller-than-modern-tabloid-size issues of *SEAC* were masterpieces of compression. Apart from the contents already noted, these were war news, items about the home front, feature articles lifted from national newspapers and readers' letters in which troops really spoke their minds. When Lady Astor, that most intolerant of do-gooders, said 'Soldiers would rather have a fried egg than a glass of beer any day,' Corporal N Ellis of 15 Independent Signals, responded: 'I suggest to Nancy Astor, a non-drinker, that she does not know her subject. Give the lads their glass of beer and make it a big 'un. If the honourable lady wants to do something for the fighting services, let her agitate for decent smokes in place of the local-made 'Woodbines' we have had to contend with for the past month.'

Every attempt was made to impart a little glamour. There was the day early in 1944 when Vera Lynn arrived in Calcutta to entertain the troops with ENSA. A *SEAC* staff reporter interviewed her 'in her hotel bedroom' and revealed that 'at Bombay she went swimming in a scanty swimming suit, one of those panties and brassiere jobs (she showed them to the Press).'

A more cultured scoop was a set of Feliks Topolski's rugged drawings of fighting soldiers on the Burma Front. The Pole was an official war artist with a unique style.

And for our last look at the content of *SEAC*, a glimpse of Frank's schooldays back in Monmouth. On August 8, 1945 his 'Good Morning' column dealt with the dropping of the first atom bomb on Japan. In the style he invented for the *Daily Express*, he starts: 'This is it, or pretty near it. This points to the end of the story. Japan is done.' Further on, 'it has ceased to be a war and has become a massacre.' He recalls speculating to his old science master: 'Will it ever be possible for one madman, by pressing a button, to blow up the world?' He was given a dusty answer: 'Young man, don't mix your political speculation with your science, which isn't too sound anyway judging by your last exam result. Incidentally, your idea is nonsense.'

Frank Owen had quickly become a man to be reckoned with in the Far East. Reg Cudlipp remarked: 'He was very much *persona grata* with Mountbatten and in consequence whenever he visited the Burma Front he was always well-received by the generals. He entered enthusiastically into the campaign of making the Forgotten Army well-remembered. His articles lifted morale and made Frank a very influential character in the Command.'

He was never in awe of generals and top staff officers at the Delhi and Kandy headquarters. Cudlipp remembers him telling an emissary with a complaint from one Delhi high-up: 'Will you give the general a message from me? Tell him to go fuck himself.' Cudlipp wondered whether the message got through in that form.

Frank got on famously with Slim after a rather cool first interview. Slim tells how the *SEAC* editor, touring his army area, had asked to see him: 'A hefty-looking

Journal of the

DEKHO!

Burma Star Association

Spring 1979   Issue No. 82

The magazine Frank edited for the post-war Burma Star boys

second lieutenant was ushered into my office . . . I had strong views on Service newspapers and sat the young man down for ten minutes while I explained to him how his paper should be run and what were an editor's duties. He listened very politely, said he would do his best, saluted and left. It was only after he had gone that I learned he had been one of the youngest and most brilliant editors in Fleet Street.'

Slim made complete amends, calling *SEAC* 'the best wartime Service journal I have seen', adding: 'It – and Owen himself – made no mean contribution to our morale.'

Supply from the air was the secret of recapture of Burma. When Major General Frank Messervy's 7th Indian Division was cut off during the second Arakan campaign in February 1944, Dakota bombers – the workhorses of World War II – flew 714 sorties to deliver 2,300 tons of ammunition, food, mail and bundles of *SEAC* printed on the morning of the drop.

Similarly the paper was delivered to beleaguered Kohima and Imphal and to Major General Wingate's Chindit brigades who had been deliberately dropped behind Japanese lines.

George Angell, a Herefordian Chindit, says: 'We could never have survived without the air drops and the pinpoint accuracy of the air crews. They supplied us with everything. I wanted a new pair of jungle boots. It arrived just like a postal packet would in Civvy Street. I remember trying on the boots and thinking one was a bad fit – until I discovered a carefully wrapped monocle put in the toe for safety. My officer, Major Bernard Fergusson, had broken his monocle and there was the replacement.

'And as important as anything were the copies of *SEAC* that helped keep us sane and in touch. There we were in the clammy jungle, fighting mosquitos, leeches and other horrible little things like Japs, who stood between us and our own troops. Yet we were able to see what Jane was taking off and read about a world back there that was normal. It helped a lot.'

In his pre-war flirtings with the military mind Frank had talked often to the unorthodox Wingate whose theories of guerrilla warfare were in advance of his time. Only a couple of months after Frank arrived in the Far East, Wingate was killed in an air crash along with two old Fleet Street hands, the *Daily Herald*'s Stanley Wills and Stuart Emeny of the *News Chronicle*.

London journalists kept turning up, some even from combat units. Frank Owen's old *Daily Express* mate, Bob Findlay, remembers how, 'as a fighting major in the Indian Army' he used to go to Calcutta on leave from the Arakan Front to meet his fellow-hacks and be entertained in the red light district. 'The food was first-class,' said Findlay.

Frank's influence grew. As we saw earlier, Mountbatten sent him home to project the 14th Army in Britain. In Calcutta, his trenchant opinions were freely dispensed on a staff level. More senior officers like Philip Joubert, Mike Wardell and Charles Eade, the former *Sunday Dispatch* editor, were all employed on morale and propaganda duties but it was Frank who had the ear of Lord Louis.

Occasionally he lost a trick. Mountbatten's biographer, Philip Ziegler, recounts how General Sir Philip Christison was poised to attack Akyab in Arakan before the press corps was in position. 'Owen, conscious of the

Pete Rees, the Pocket General

need for publicity for the Command's first seaborne expedition, urged delay. Mountbatten seconded his efforts and signalled Christison that a cyclone threatened. But Christison pushed ahead to total military success but little publicity.'

As often as he could Frank Owen forsook the safety of Calcutta for the sharp end of the conflict. He had always cultivated military 'originals' like Wavell and Wingate, Fuller and Slim. Now he met a fellow-Welshman, Pete Rees, the busiest and most pugnacious front line general of World War II.

Rees, a son of the manse, came out of the Great War at 21 with a DSO and MC and went on to a brilliant Indian Army career. He led a brigade at Keren in the

1941 Eritrean campaign and commanded the 10th Indian Division in Iraq and against Rommel in the Western Desert. He returned to India to train and command a brand new division, the 19th 'Dagger', which was to be the shock force of Slim's massive 1945 offensive. Rees was Picton to Slim's Wellington. The two tempestuous Celts met in the build-up area. Frank Owen, 6ft 2in, gazed down on Major-General Thomas Wynford Rees (his proper name) who was a perky 5ft 2in. But there is no doubt who dominated their meeting: Pete, the man of action. He had great gifts. He had made a name as a Sandhurst instructor; he could, according to his chief staff officer, John Masters, speak Urdu, Marathi, Pushtu, Burmese and Tamil in addition to his native Welsh; he was a high grade staff officer.

But Pete Rees's greatest attribute was courage. 'I saw the small, intense figure of the General prowling in the firing line,' wrote one correspondent. He was twice wounded in World War II and won a bar to his DSO.

The role of the Dagger Division was hush hush before the Commander-in-Chief threw it into battle. There was no story for Frank's newspapers – yet. Then the Dagger was unsheathed. In a glorious fortnight Rees achieved the breakthrough which was to transform the Burma Front. Making an accelerated advance from the Singu bridgehead, his Gurkha, Rajputana and Baluchi troops with attached British battalions, including the Welch Regiment, stormed down the east bank of the Irrawady. The division advanced 18 miles in 24 hours over difficult country to reach the suburbs of Mandalay. Steadily they assaulted the 700ft hill dominating the city and then stormed Fort Dufferin, meantime sending a flying column of Ghurkas 40 miles to Maymo, cutting the Mandalay-Lashio road. On March 20 Mandalay was totally in 14th Army hands.

Slim described in his autobiography how he heard singing during the battle and came upon Rees, 'his uniform sweat-soaked and dirty, his distinguishing red scarf rumpled round his neck, his bush hat at a jaunty angle, his arm beating time, surrounded by a group of Assamese soldiers whom he was vigorously leading in the singing of Welsh missionary hymns.

'The fact that he sang in Welsh and they in Khasi only added to the harmony. I looked on admiringly. My generals had character.'

Frank Owen cleared *SEAC*'s front page to do justice to Pete's Dagger heroes, christened him the 'Green Gremlin' and suggested he could do a great job to remind the British about the 'Forgotten Army' by flying home to make a series of triumphal speeches in South Wales. Mountbatten approved and Rees set off for his welcome in the hillsides.

Frank was to meet this mighty atom again after the war. As a *Daily Mail* roving correspondent he went out to cover the independence and partition of India. Who should be up at the sharp end but General Rees holding the line in command of the Punjab Boundary Force, two divisions strong.

He had to control a population of 75 million, including 6 million Sikhs, a warrior race who were objecting to being parcelled out between India and Pakistan. Frank wrote glowingly about the little general's control of what eventually became a hopeless situation.

12. THE RAFFLES

We liberated a wing of the Raffles Hotel
and established firm (and fluid) relations
with the boss —

Frank Owen

BY mid-1945 Mountbatten's caravan was rolling.
Kohima and Imphal had been relieved, the Arakan
mopped up, the Burma Road reopened, Mandalay and
Rangoon retaken. Next stop Singapore.

For this purpose Operation Zipper was set up to
invade Malaya with a landing force of seven 14th Army
divisions at Port Swettenham, a parachute brigade and
commando brigade to make a two-pronged attack on
Singapore Island, 500 aircraft and a fleet of battleships
and cruisers.

Frank Owen, promoted in rapid stages to lieutenant-
colonel by now, was determined his newspaper unit
would be in on the act. His advance party would go in
with the assault troops and start publishing *SEAC*
editions as soon as they could commandeer a printing
press in Singapore.

Zipper was scheduled for September 9 and the build-
up was on course when the atom bomb was dropped at
Hiroshima on August 6. On September 2 Japan's

surrender became a fact on the deck of the Mighty Mo
– the US battleship Missouri – in Tokyo Harbour.
Zipper was downgraded from an invasion to a mere
occupation landing.

But Colonel Owen still despatched his vanguard with
the first wave of troops into Singapore and within four
days *SEAC* was printed on the presses of the *Straits
Times*. In charge was Peter Eastwood, in later years
autocratic managing editor of *The Daily Telegraph*, and
his assistant Bob Jackson, a former Tanks man. *SEAC*
quickly became a crusading paper, exposing the sorts of
rackets that become rife in times of military liberation.

Frank meanwhile was commanding his main force
back at Calcutta, fast becoming a backwater. S E Asia
Command was being separated from India so it was
decided to move the entire newspaper operation to
Singapore.

The journalists were allocated space in one of the
inevitable Dakotas but they were a seat short. Frank
called over to one of the juniors, Ted Bishop, and said:
'We haven't got room for you. You'll have to make
your own way. Can you hitch a lift?'

Ted, who had not long since made the long sea voyage
around the Cape, was a bit nonplussed about this
pierhead jump. Frank was helpful: 'There's a whole
fleet of merchant ships going all the time from
Kiddapore Docks. Find one of them.'

'So I went down to the docks,' Ted recalls, 'and
started hailing ships to ask: "Can you take me to
Singapore?" No luck until I came across a rank old
coal-burning tramp called the Fort Stager. The first
mate said: "We're weighing first thing in the morning.
The old man's legless in his bunk, but if you turn up in

the morning you can ask him. If I were you I'd bring a couple of bottles of Scotch because he's run out.''

'So I went back to Frank and put it to him. He knew how: "To my knowledge the Yanks have plenty of Scotch in their mess and they're short of beer. Give me your beer coupons and I'll trade.'' He was soon back, handed me two bottles and said: "There's your fare.'' The tramp's skipper was happy and off we sailed, but he still made me work. He put a shovel in my hand and showed me the stokehole. I worked my passage to Singapore.'

Ted was puzzled when he stepped on the quay. He had no idea where the newspaper unit was. He was in a strange city and there were still Japanese sentries on the harbour gates. He walked past them. The only place in Singapore he had heard of was the Raffles Hotel.

'I hailed a rickshaw,' Ted said, 'and told the jin to take me to the Raffles, where I asked if anyone had heard of Frank Owen. They sent me straight to the third floor where I found a massive party in full flood with Frank dominating the proceedings.

'He had a vicious-looking samurai sword in his hands. "Hello, young Bishop,'' he bellowed. "Just in time to help me show how the Japs did their beheading with a weapon like this. Kneel down.'' And he proceeded to whirl it around the region of my neck and head. Welcome to Singapore, I thought.'

Once established in the Malay Peninsula, Frank Owen started to go flyabout, hitching lifts in military aircraft. One day they lost touch with his plane. Eastwood mobilised the cub reporter. 'He's missing up country.' Bishop was told. 'Grab a car. Go and find Frank Owen, wherever he is.'

Young Ted eventually tracked down his editor in a jungle clearing about 60 miles north of the Singapore Causeway. 'What are you doing here?' – 'I've come to rescue you' – 'No need. I'm quite happy talking to these chaps.' And Frank turned round to resume his chat with a group of local villagers.

No doubt he found background and contacts in such conversations for his post-war roving reporter activities, but his obsession was still for the 14th Army. As Anna Phillips shrewdly observed. 'I am sure Frank's years in South East Asia were the most rewarding of his life. He simply seemed to be cut out to give his life to a cause and without it he was lost. The cause of the 14th Army set his adrenalin flowing like nothing else. Why? He was for one thing very male-orientated. His pals, I'm sure, meant a great deal more to him than any of his many amours, including myself.'

Frank's championship of the Burma troops comes out very clearly in a letter sent from Singapore to Michael Foot on October 6, 1945. Earlier that year War Minister Sir James Grigg had upset Mountbatten's Malayan invasion plans by allowing troops to return to Britain after 40 months Far East service instead of 44. This was done without consultation and, suspiciously, on the brink of the General Election which Churchill's Tories lost. Frank, along with many Burma hands, considered they had been used as political pawns.

He wrote to Foot: 'Really, it was a serious situation here and there might have been real trouble if any more injustice had been done our troops. I said to Bill Slim of (new Labour War Minister) Lawson: "If the other bugger, Target For Next Year Grigg, had come, you would have needed a guard with fixed bayonets to

6 Oct. 1945

SOUTH EAST ASIA COMMAND HEADQUARTERS.

Dear Mike.

No Letters Ever Arrive Anywhere, has been my alibi for years & now is (unexpectedly) proven. I have letters returned to me from London. Naturally, it is LA Maclaren who is involved. I hope you will underline this point for me when you see her, & point out that this exonerates me for the next five years. I am looking forward to Tribune, with one moan. Really, it was a serious situation here, & there might have been real trouble if any more injustice had been done our troops. I said to Bill Slim of Lawson (who did v. well) "If the other bugger, Target For Next Year Grigg, had come you would have needed a guard with fixed bayonets to protect him" Bill replied "Yes, & to pick the guard very carefully, too."

So we are very pleased with the Labour Govt, & correspondingly disgusted with Lord Beaverbrook. I got Blue Graham to send a story on 14th Army feeling about the matter. The world's greatest newspaper did not use a line, tho it represented the opinions of several hundred thousand British citizens who had fought for their fucking empire.

I've been to Singapore, Hong Kong, Saigon etc. We entered with the assault troops all ready to shoot, & being pelted with flowers. We liberated a wing of the Raffles Hotel, (about the best in Asia) & established,

Greetings for Mike Foot from Singapore

protect him.'' Bill replied: "Yes, and to pick the guard very carefully, too.''

Frank's old employer, Beaverbrook, also got a broadside: 'So we are very pleased with the Labour Government and correspondingly disgusted with Lord Beaverbrook.' The letter recounts how Frank had persuaded Clive Graham (*Express war* correspondent and post-war racing tipster, The Scout) to send a story home about the 14th Army's feelings.

But, 'the World's Greatest Newspaper did not use a line, though it represented the opinions of several hundred thousand British citizens who had fought for their fucking Empire.' Clearly such disillusion must have helped steer Frank Owen from Beaverbrook Newspapers to the *Daily Mail* on demob but there may have been other factors (as we shall see).

Politics apart, the *SEAC* journalists were having a rip-roaring time. He tells Foot: 'We liberated a wing of the Raffles Hotel (about the best in Asia) and established firm (and fluid) relations with the boss, who also owns the biggest brewery in Malaya and incidentally the *Straits Times*, on whose presses we produced 12,000 *SEAC*'s, to his astonishment.

'We then rushed to a Jap camp, where the bastards were still under arms but much bewildered, and looted three fine cars, a Cadillac, a Dodge and a Hudson. Most generals are still driving around in Jeeps.'

SEAC's leading articles had been model ones: 'What Singapore needs is orderly government. We must return to normal . . .' One leader, wrote Frank 'which attacked "military jackanapes in uniform" was especially welcomed by the civilian sahibs, who gave us a hell of a fine Chinese dinner to mark approval of our liberal attitude.'

Frank Owen's last task for Mountbatten was to write a 176-page official history which was published by HM Stationery Office in 1946 under the title, *The Campaign in Burma*. The book was written in Singapore − twice. He lost his first completed manuscript, the only copy, and had to do the whole job again, according to Ted Bishop.

It is solid military history but contains graphic episodes. This description of the 1942 retreat from Burma shows Frank at his best: 'An army is moving along a jungle track. The sun has sunk behind the trees, and shadows hem in the procession. The step is not lively, nor is it easy to keep, for the soldiers' footfalls make no sound in the dust that lies deep upon the road . . . The soldiers feel dust, they breathe it and they would swallow it if they did not keep their mouths shut . . .

'Review the troops as they approach. Red eyes, grey faces, beards, their shirts torn with jungle thorns, striped black with tonight's wet sweat and white with yesterday's dried salt of sweat . . . Dirt and blood stain the rags that bind their wounds. They have been marching with short halts for the past 24 hours, and there has been no time to wash, even if there was water. These soldiers are marching towards another battle.'

When the last copy of *SEAC* was published on May 15, 1946, Frank Owen had already gone home to see his campaign history off the press. Then, on to a demob suit, a half-colonel's gratuity and an OBE − for which

On pages following:
The last copy of SEAC — 15 May 1946

SEAC

All-Services Daily Newspaper
Of S. E. Asia Command
Published for the last time
at 127 Cecil St., S'pore
Printed by the "Straits
Times" Press
No. 852. Wednesday, 15 May 1946.
5 cts. Malaya, Ceylon: 10 cts.
Hong Kong: 1 anna India
and Burma.

.... Good Night

Today we of SEAC complete a high duty; today, too, we relinquish a high privilege. We have tried to measure up to the first; we have tried in grateful humility to use the second wisely, and avoid the temptations which great power puts before men.

This newspaper was born in the liberality of mind of its sponsor, Admiral Mountbatten. As he tells in the adjacent column, it was conceived as one of the psychological foundations of the new-born South East Asia Command in the late summer of '43.

The project was just one expression of a policy of leadership which has been proved over and over again. Keep the men informed, keep them in the picture. Explain, explain, explain.

It has been said that one of the supreme qualities of a leader —or a business executive—is the choice of men to carry out policy. Mountbatten chose Owen—a choice hardly calculated to bring him great popularity in certain very powerful quarters, a choice that needed courage. Owen has been called every name in politics, but no-one has ever accused him of twisting the news.

When the paper was born, on 10 January, 1944, there was much still to be done before the world could regard itself as on the road to Victory. In Asia the Jap was still on top. Britain, America, were still on the defensive.

At Comilla little-known Lieut. General William Slim was commanding a force then charged with keeping the Jap out of India. That force was already the biggest of the British Imperial armies but it was unnamed. The words "Fourteenth Army" were Top Secret.

There was a feeling among the men that there, on the borders of Burma, they were unheeded, unsung, forgotten by the people at Home.

Owen sent a cable to Premier Churchill just before SEAC published its first issue, asking him for a message of cheer to the Fourteenth Army. The message came in time for issue No. 2. It was published. The censors were apoplectic. Owen went strangely bland Could we censor the Prime Minister? he asked. Correspondents cabled the story all over the world. Fourteenth Army was on the map. From that time on, SEAC forged ahead with two main objects. First, to bring to the men of Fourteenth Army and its supporting air forces, British and American, news of Home; then to take to the people of the world news of the Fourteenth Army.

This was the first inter-Services newspaper in any command, anywhere. Its staff, from the beginning, was drawn

We are used to reading different newspapers and we have very varied tastes and opinions so it was obvious that the paper would have to carry light articles and serious articles, frivolous cartoons and general knowledge tests, and sports news.

Most important of all it would have to be edited as fairly and impartially as possible, and it would have to be our own paper, in which we could air our views and discuss them among ourselves. All this would have been comparatively easy with an unlimited paper supply, but as we should certainly be limited to four pages, the attainment of all these objects presented quite a problem.

From scratch

I decided that the man to solve the problem was Frank Owen. When I managed to trace him, he had just blossomed from a trooper RAC into a fully-fledged cadet, and was with difficulty persuaded to abandon his ambition to be a Second Lieutenant in a tank, in order to come out here as a desk-wallah and run a daily newspaper. Eventually, however, his resistance was overcome and he arrived in Calcutta to start 'SEAC' from scratch.

The original staff consisted of Lieutenant Ian Coster, of the Royal Marines (one P(o senior to his Editor). Leading Telegraphist Len Jackson of the Royal Navy, Cpl. Tom W'cox, RAC. Sgt. H. V. Tillotson, RAF. Pte. George Chisholm, RASC, and Cpl. H. Stainforth, RAF. Eventually they collected around them the team which was to make SEAC an important factor in our daily lives out here.

I told Frank Owen what I needed. I authorised the Editorial Staff to express their own opinions in the "Good Morning" column or in reply to correspondence, but on no account to inject them into other parts of the paper. And in January 1944 I wrote to SEAC myself, saying that one of the objects we were fighting the Axis for was freedom of opinion and expression. In two and a half years I have never once had to interfere in the policy of the paper, or remind those who were producing it of my wishes.

Wot—no Brig!

I am glad to say that neither SEAC nor its Staff has escaped criticism—it would have had to be very dull and lifeless to do that. The paper has hardly got going when a question was asked in Parliament about how long Frank Owen had been in the Army, and why he had been promoted Brigadier. Owen, who had been in two years, and had reached the exalted rank of Second Lieutenant, was delighted to find that SEAC was already on the map.

Only two serious complaints ...

Supremo's Farew

Message To SE

When I was instructed at the Quebec Co August 1943, to create an inter-service, inter-allie to be known as the South East Asia Command, I : among the most urgent points to be dealt with, for an inter-service daily newspaper.

I knew that if we were to fight a campaign duration, thousands of miles away, we should all that we were still in touch, not only with what w; in the world at large, but also with what was home.

nad with Soldiers. Airmen—both Brit: mean—during two years of visits to areas, I have inv how SEAC was g has been clear answers that they did myself.

It is on behalf of have been read: throughout the who of South East As: to thank Frank O gallant team for job.

Louis M

'CONTACT
GOOD-BYE

This week's iss.' GHQ(I)'s weekly carries this farewe.

Many men now i mand knew SEA newspaper which. were battling in the bad old days, kept with news of the own and other fro was happening at

Wherever Brit's! fought it out aga SEAC was to be those cut off g through SEAC.

Now SEAC is terday it went thro ing press for the la

It was always fo: men who went thro and the heat of b had as its guiding Owen, former edito Evening Standard, writer and an outs nalist. Under him many sound, practi whom we knew in days of pre-1939.

Housi
to co:

LONDON, 1 London is envisag involved in the c presented this we annual estimates

The grand total t one amount of £7,6 acquisition of land ment to deal with situation and a c of £7,387,000 as sum to cover the further development

A sum of £3.21 additional housing purchase of land is

...vell
...AC

...ference in ... command, ...ade a note, ...of the need

...f indefinite ...need to feel ...happening ...ing on at

...Sailors and ...sh and Ame- ...and a half ...the forward ...ertainly asked ...ing down. It ...from their ...got as much ...xing it as I

...all of us who ...is of SEAC ...cle 5,000 miles ...that I want ...en and his ...a magnificent

---

' SAYS
: TO US

...r of Contact, ...newspaper, ...! to SEAC:— ...n India Com- ...C, the daily ...when they ...jungle in the ...hem supplied ...war on their ...is and what ...ome.

...Servicemen ...ist the Japs. ...und. Even ...t the news

...ore, for ves- ...gh the print- ...ist time. ...tunate in the ...ough the mail ...making it. It ...star Frank ...r of London's ...a brilliant ...tanding jour- ...there were ...cal craftsmen ...the faraway

---

London
will say it
with flags

LONDON, Tues.—Flagpoles are going up, steel barriers are being erected and lamp standards are being painted in the parts of London along which the two columns—one marching and other mechanised—will travel on V-Day.

Tubular steel barriers for police control purposes are being erected at Marble Arch, Parliament-square and Trafalgar-square.

Opposite Marlborough-gate in the Mall, where the King will take the salute, scaffolding for the saluting base has already been erected, and flagpoles for 103 flags of the British Dominions and the Allies, which will fly from both sides of the Mall are being placed in position.

Lamp standards in Trafalgar-square have been painted bright silver.

The LCC's proposal to spend £28,000 on Victory celebrations will be considered at today's meeting of the Council.—Reuter.

20 DIV DISBANDS

NEW DELHI, Tues.—One of the most famous divisions of Four-teenth Army, the 20th Indian Division, has now been disbanded.

Raised in Bangalore in 1942, the division had only one com-mander, Maj.-Gen. Douglas Gracey, now Lieutenant-General commanding 15th Indian Corps.

Awards to the division, which fought in Burma from 1942 to the end, included two VCs, 26 DSOs, and 152 MCs.

...ng in London
st £15,000,000

...ues.—A £15,000,000 rehousing plan for ...ed by the LCC, and details of the huge sums ...ifferent aspects of the scheme are to be ...ek when the Council meets to consider the

...made up of ...13,000 for the ...and develop- ...the housing ...cond amount ...provisional ...purchase of ...schemes. ...1,500 for the

...covers the provision of homes on block dwelling and cottage es-tates, construction of roads and reinstatement after war damage of various block dwelling estates.

The additional £7,387,000 pro-vides among other things for de-velopment of Hainault, Kidbrooke Park, Loughton and other cot-tage estates and for the build-

---

THE BIG-FOUR WRANGLE

MOLOTOV GETS
AN 'ULTIMATUM'

PARIS, Tues.—State Secretary James Byrnes tonight proposed that when discussion of Germany is ended, the Foreign Ministers' Council should adjourn until 15 June, and suggested that the Peace conference be opened either on 1 July or 15 July.

He delivered a virtual ultima-tum that the Council must set the date for the Peace Confer-ence at the resumed meeting on 15 June or else evolve an entirely new mechanism for the peace treaties.

The proposals will be dis-cussed tomorrow. The impres-sion here is that the Council is prepared to break up after three weeks of fruitless wrangling.

Russian Foreign Minister Molotov offered to pull out from Bulgaria Russian troops, said to be holding the lines of communi-cations to Austria, if the United States and Britain would agree to similar action in Italy.

Molotov's offer was made con-tingent on the insertion in the Italian peace treaty of a clause requiring that all United States and British troops be withdrawn from Italy as soon as the treaty is signed.

Foreign Secretary Ernest Bevin replied that if the Council could start discussing Austria at once —and could reach an agreement on the withdrawal of all troops from that country, including Russian—the problem would be solved automatically, as there would be no need of troops' hold-ing the L of C.

Molotov opposes

Byrnes approved this sugges-tion, and proposed the drafting of the peace treaty with Austria. Molotov opposed on the grounds that the Ministers had been struggling for months on five treaties without reaching an agreement.

He said it would merely further hamper the talks to add an-other treaty to the agenda.

At this morning's session on the Italian treaty, the Big Four appeared, after 19 days of gruel-ling debate, to be as deadlocked as ever. They failed to find a definite form for colonial or re-parations issues, which once seemed near solution.

The only basis for optimism is that neither Russia nor the Western Powers want to bear the responsibility for admitting that the conference has failed. All the participants seemed grimly determined not to give up while the faintest prospect of success remains.—U.P.

LESNEVICH
BEATS MILLS

LONDON, Tues.—In Harringay arena, Gus Lesnevich won the world cruiserweight champion-ship, beating Freddie Mills. The referee stopped the contest in the tenth round of the scheduled fifteen rounds.

Both men gave and took much punishment throughout the fight. By the seventh round, Mills appeared as strong as ever, getting in some telling blows. He was boxing superbly in the

---

Dutch are
moving into
Bandoeng

BATAVIA, Tues.—Dutch troops are today handing over to Dutch troops the control of Bandoeng hill station, 100 miles south-east of Batavia, Dutch sources in Bandoeng reported.

While the handing over was going on serious clashes between Dutch forces and Indonesian extremists occurred outside the town.

British guns broke up a body of Indonesians who had caused ten casualties—two of them fatal—to the Dutch in an attack with rifles and machine-guns near Tjitaroem, south-west of Bandoeng.

Stolen rubber exported

A Dutch report today from Medan, on the east coast of Sumatra, claimed that Indone-stans have exported from Sumatra to Malaya a large quantity of rubber stolen from local plantations.

The Dutch destroyer Van Galen took part in a combined operation with a Netherlands Army detachment against a 'pirate stronghold' on the south-coast of Borneo, a Netherlands Navy announcement stated to-day.—Reuter.

U.S. Kills Rumour

No 'better'
atom bomb

NEW YORK, Tues.—A joint announcement by the Army and Navy said that the United States had not got a more powerful atom-ic bomb than that dropped on Nagasaki, Japan, last year, a Washington despatch to the New York Times reported today.

This announcement answered rumours abroad that the United States had developed a bomb with a more devastating energy.

Vice-Admiral W. H. P. Blandy, Commander of the atomic bomb task force, told a press conference on the eve of his departure for the Pacific that although the fullest possible story of the des-truction of the fleet of 97 "guinea pig" ships in the Bikini Atoll this July would be made public, certain specific points would not be disclosed.—Reuter and U.P.

'LIFERS' FOR
AIDING ENEMY

LONDON, Tues.—Two British

he had to wait nine years. By error another Colonel H F Owen picked up the regalia. In 1955 this officer wrote to the War Office saying: 'You've given me an OBE. What about a pension?' The War Office investigated, discovered the error, ordered the other colonel to return the insignia and apologised to Frank who had long past forgotten all about it. A package duly arrived by post with a letter from the Queen: 'This is the insignia my father should have presented to you.'

13. MAIL — AND FAREWELL

His friends, who watched him a few years
ago painting red streaks across the true-
blue face of Lord Beaverbrook's Evening
Standard, will watch with delighted
apprehension his impact on the house of
Rothermere —

The Manchester Guardian

FOR about half this century the *Daily Mail* was a paper in search of an editor. About a score of assorted bottoms warmed the chair of power from the departure of Tommy Marlowe, Northcliffe's henchman, about 1920 to the arrival of David English 50 years later.

Frank Owen was among the short-lived 20. It was an open Fleet Street secret during the Hitler War that Esmond, second Lord Rothermere, had offered the *Mail* to Frank. Within weeks of demob he was on the Harmsworth payroll, firmly snubbing Beaverbrook whose crackling tinder box he had been through the 30s and into the 40s.

Why did he do it? Not for money. The Beaver had supplemented his pay handsomely while he was in the Army and would have over-matched any Rothermere offer. Perhaps it was because he was upset by the *Express*'s indifference to the 14th Army (as expressed in his bitter Singapore letter to Foot). Perhaps it was the opportunity to edit a national morning paper. With Arthur Christiansen firmly in the saddle, there was no chance of the *Daily Express*.

In a 1980 broadcast, Ludovic Kennedy recalled the Beaverbrook-Mountbatten feud which arose from a scene in the wartime film *In Which We Serve*. It lampooned the *Express*'s headline: There will be no war this year. Amid other disclosures Kennedy cited the fact that Ian Coster, who had worked for Mountbatten's Command publications, lost his *Express* job for this reason after returning from the Far East. Kennedy suggests this was why Frank went to the *Mail*. I would doubt it. The Beaver had too much regard for Frank to do that and in any case grabbed him back like a prodigal son when he quit Northcliffe House.

Whatever the reasons, the front page of the *Mail* of July 4, 1946 carried a prominent puff: At the top the 'Good Morning!' logo in Frank's handwriting which had introduced his *SEAC* leaders. Next in capital 24 point sans serif type, FRANK OWEN JOINS THE MAIL. The text outlined his career and ended: 'Owen is a newspaperman with a vigorous and independent mind. His views may not always be those of his newspaper. But they will interpret honestly the thoughts and feelings of men who fought overseas and whose job will be to rebuild Britain.'

Frank bustled round Britain and the world, bombarding his readers with ideas they had never seen before in the *Mail*. He backed the Beveridge welfare reforms, the Bevan health programme and nationalisation, particularly of the pits.

A year or two later Frank explained: 'When Lord

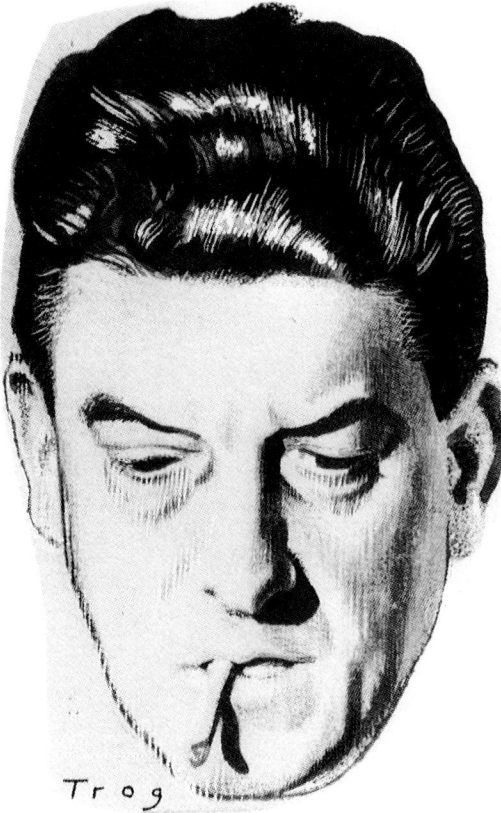

Good ~~July 4/1946~~
Morning!

FRANK OWEN JOINS THE DAILY MAIL

FRANK OWEN, former Fleet-street editor, a journalist with an international reputation, comes back to Fleet-street from five years in the Army.

After serving as a trooper he was commissioned in the Royal Armoured Corps. He went to the Far East with Admiral Lord Louis Mountbatten in 1943, ending his service there as lieutenant-colonel.

In Burma Owen ran the jungle newspaper *SEAC*. His outspoken daily column "Good Morning" was read by a million men of the once forgotten Fourteenth Army.

Now Frank Owen and his column "Good Morning" have been demobilised from the Army. They have joined *The Daily Mail.*

Owen is a newspaperman with a vigorous and independent mind. His views may not always be those of this newspaper.

But they will interpret honestly the thoughts and feelings of men who fought overseas and whose job now on returning home will be to rebuild Britain.

Good Morning!

**begins
in tomorrow's
Daily Mail**

Frank joins The Mail, *July 1946 — Trog's caricature made a smoker of a man who seldom touched cigarettes . . .*

113

Frank takes Bill Slim to a London Press Club luncheon for the generals who won the war — October 1946

Rothermere discussed with me before the General Election of 1945 my coming to the *Daily Mail*, I told him that I had been for 20 years a supporter of the nationalisation of the mines. And I wanted the freedom to be that on the *Mail*.

'In one of my early personal columns on July 12, 1946, I mentioned that Lord Northcliffe himself had advocated the nationalisation of the mines 30 years previously. From then onwards that column reeked of coal dust. Three or four times most of it dealt with nothing else and almost every two or three weeks the subject recurred. I rejoiced that the miners were getting a fair deal at last.'

As early as January 1947 he filled the editorial chair in the absence of Stanley Horniblow. When the editor returned, Frank made a trip to Asia where the Indian sub-continent was on the brink of splitting up into the self-governing units of India, Pakistan, Ceylon and Burma.

On March 4 Frank Owen became *Daily Mail* editor, a popular choice among the journalists. Edward Pickering (later *Daily Express* editor and top *Times* Newspapers executive) was his managing editor, a kind of nuts and bolts man, an adjutant who looks after detail while the editor takes the larger horizon.

Sir Edward told me: 'Frank's arrival brought a great gust of fresh air into the office. In no department was this more apparent than in the leader-writing. George Murray had been an excellent leader-writer for many years – within the confines of a somewhat stuffy *Mail* tradition. Suddenly, with Frank's inspiring three o'clock leader conferences, George was writing pieces that were the political banners of the late Forties.

'Each afternoon Frank, George and I would meet to discuss subjects of the day. Whatever the chosen topic Frank would immediately put on a firework display – lively ideas, apposite anecdotes drawn from his fine memory for political history, phrases that made headlines, introductions or pay-offs. George Murray absorbed it all, translated it into immaculate English and the *Mail* leaders, now transferred to Column One, Page One, became the talk of the political world.'

But Frank Owen made a greater contribution. He knew how to inspire a staff, said Pickering, and bring in new, young talent. George Elam, a 40-year *Mail* man who finished as picture editor, underlined this. George, a humble photographer under the Owen regime, recalled: 'I remember him as a gigantic, flamboyant character full of the joys of spring. I can't recall him being nasty to anyone on the staff. He was one of the boys, a lovely man to work with. He was perpetually on the editorial floor, not one of those remote editors you occasionally bumped into in the lift. He drank with everyone else in the office pubs like Auntie's and the Mucky Duck.'

The globetrotting continued. Early in 1948 Frank made a six-week tour of the United States and broadcast four times about British attitudes and policies. In the September of that year he flew to South Africa where Prime Minister Daniel Malan refused to be interviewed by him. That the arch-apostle of apartheid should decline to see him was a compliment to Frank Owen's vehement liberal views and the power of his questioning.

There were occasional clashes with Associated Newspapers management. Soon after Frank's return from

South Africa, there were reports that he had walked out after a policy row but Rothermere, in a cable from France, made a complete denial and one periodical was forced to publish a correction. But tempests there were. A stormy petrel seldom nests happily with pouter pigeons.

Eventually, after little more than three years in the editorial chair, Frank was out. On May 24, 1950, Associated announced that they and their editor had parted company 'by mutual agreement'. He was 45 and had lost his last executive job. Yorkshireman Guy Schofield, editor of the same group's *Evening News*, took over.

Frank had made a powerful enemy, Rothermere's second wife, Ann. One office rumour was that this was a case of hell hath no fury . . . She had fancied Frank and been rejected, the gossips said. She certainly had a roving nature and left Rothermere for the James Bond thriller writer, Ian Fleming, a year or two later and married him.

Anna Phillips discounts any sex entanglement between the boss's wife and Frank, who certainly wasn't Lady Rothermere's fan by the time he left. 'Her ladyship', says Anna, 'was always meddling in company politics. Stewart MacLean, her appointee as managing director of the *Mail*, was the cause of Frank's departure and, with hindsight, I think she regretted her interference in the newspaper. Of the two there was little to choose between her and MacLean as the target of Frank's justified resentment. Before that, she and Frank were on good terms.'

Two quotations, three years apart, from the American *Time* magazine are interesting. **March, 1947:**

'Mailmen gossiped that Owen's promotion was plotted by Ann Rothermere, who keeps a bright and calculating eye on her easy-going husband's affairs.'

June, 1950: 'It has long been common knowledge in Fleet Street that the real boss (of the *Mail*) wears a petticoat . . . Without consulting Editor Owen, she (Ann) often summoned staffers to her home to assign stories or suggest new features . . . Overbearing, tight-pursed (managing) director McLean moved in on editorial authority, in some cases firing, shuffling and promoting without consulting Owen . . . In recent months eight top editorial executives and writers and two directors have been fired or quit. Last week Frank Owen quit.'

In letters she wrote earlier in 1950, Lady Harmsworth describes her intrigues to launch a gossip column and accuses Frank Owen of 'doing a quiet, efficient job of sabotage.'

Another theory is that (pardon the mixed metaphor) Frank Owen was torpedoed by a 26-year-old red herring. Just three months before he left the *Mail* there had been a General Election on February 23. Attlee's Labour, defending their head-to-head 1945 landslide majority of 196 over the Tories, were in a distinctly nervous state as they faced a disillusioned country.

As parties do in such crises, they went for the jugular. Back in 1924 when Ramsay MacDonald's first Labour Government was outed, Attlee wrote in his memoirs, 'the *Daily Mail* produced a letter alleged to have been written by Zinoviev, the Soviet Foreign Secretary, the implication of which was that the Labour Party was very much the same as the Communists. The matter was very badly handled by MacDonald and lost Labour many votes.'

In 1950 Labour dredged up the Red Letter smear and used it against its original perpetrators. In a party political broadcast six days before the poll, deputy prime minister Herbert Morrison said: 'The electoral tactic of stunt and scare is very much ingrained in the Tory Party machine. Stunts and scares are a form of cheating.'

The *Mail* took a lot of stick in these propaganda exchanges and Frank Owen could well have been blamed for not defending his paper's record more vigorously. As it turned out, Labour held on with only 16 more seats than the Conservatives and in a new political climate Rothermere might have preferred to employ a less radical editor.

Reginald Cudlipp, *News of the World* editor at that time and an old *SEAC* comrade, told me: 'At the *Mail* Frank never made the grade as we all expected. He continued to write forceful pieces but I don't think he was out to be an editor, especially of the slim sheets we had to turn out after the war.'

But on the *Mail* editorial floor Edward Pickering was one of many to regret parting with their chief. 'It was too brief a reign,' he said, 'and I remember it with total admiration. He was a brilliant shooting star and, for me, the afterglow still remains.'

14. THREE YEARS HARD

'Begin at the beginning,' the King said,
gravely, 'and go on till you come to the end;
then stop.' —

Alice in Wonderland

IT was a very different Frank Owen who rejoined the
Daily Express in June 1950, very different from the
carefree spirit who had left the paper a dozen years
before to edit the *Standard*. Anna Phillips, who had
parted from her husband in 1945 and divorced him two
years later, was back with Frank and noticed the
change. 'He was suffering from paranoia,' she said.
'His personality had begun to break up.'

On the *Mail*, for the first time, Frank had been forced
to watch his back. His boss there, Rothermere, was no
Beaverbrook with a crusader's shield to protect his
favourites.

Frank became an *Express* columnist and roving
reporter. He covered the Malayan guerrilla war against
the Communists and had other assignments but seldom
now wrote with the snap and conviction that had been
his hallmark.

Beaverbrook, meanwhile, had bought the Lloyd
George papers for £15,000 from the Countess, the

Welsh Wizard's second wife and longtime mistress. Here was a treasure chest into which Beaverbrook could dip and indulge his hobby of researching recent political history. After casting round among other names – including that of US dramatist Robert Sherwood – his lordship finally dropped on Frank Owen to write a massive – and intendedly important – life of Lloyd George entitled *Tempestuous Journey.*

It was a bizarre operation from start to finish. Anna, on the payroll as secretary and typist, described how she and Frank were quartered in a 'gloomy, cavernous room off a small alleyway behind the *Standard* building.' Frank was kept firmly to a regular quota of words like a schoolboy in detention. The only light relief came when a certain Colonel Wintle used to call in, flashing his glass eye and monocle. Wintle, briefly notorious for debagging a solicitor alleged to have cheated him, sought out Frank as one of those boozy acquaintances who had listened to his tale.

But there was scant welcome for the colonel. Frank was under the cosh, supervised by three bosses – Countess Lloyd George who did some of the research and kept her horny husband's reputation pristine, newspaper executive Sir Thomas Marlow cracking the word-flow whip and Beaverbrook reading every word and 'suggesting' frequent revisions.

Eventually in 1954 *Tempestuous Journey* appeared in the bookshops. It ran to the best part of 800 pages and carried Frank's name as author. He had done the job on salary, not on a royalty basis, which was perhaps lucky for him. In a brief introduction he wrote: 'For three years I have quarried in the vast papers of the Lloyd George Archives which now belong to Lord Beaver-

The Happy Warrior!

brook. There are 1,025 boxes of them . . .' (this probably written with heartfelt thanks that the great grind of composition was at last ended).

Frank added: 'These papers were placed at my disposal and I have to thank Lord Beaverbrook for that . . . I acknowledge, too, the access which Lord Beaverbrook allowed me to his own papers.' Thanks, boss!

The author was dispatched around the country and to Dublin, whipping up sales but only one impression was printed. The book fell between two stools: It was too long and detailed for the general reader and too journalistic a job to impress those academics who specialised in Lloyd George studies. Canadian Professor Don M Cregier, who had spent 20 years researching Lloyd George's pre-World War I career, called the Owen book 'flashy and overblown' while many years later Nottingham Professor Chris Wrigley called it a 'lively account but limited in its choice of themes'.

According to A J P Taylor's Beaverbrook biography, the great man was dissatisfied with the final version, 'not surprisingly since it was a rush job . . . (which) only scratched at the surface of the vast material'. Surely this was Beaverbrook's own fault. He had ordained the method.

Seldom in *Tempestuous Journey* does Frank Owen reveal any personal view or anecdote of the statesman to whom he was 'apprenticed' in the late 1920s. The most revealing section concerns Lloyd George's treacherous treatment of Major David Davies who had acted as his political eyes and ears during critical periods of World War I, yet was instantly discarded when he brought back unwelcome news

– a case of shooting the messenger.

Frank Owen wrote: 'He (Lloyd George) could be coldly indifferent to old colleagues who had served him loyally and well . . . This man with the most compelling personal charm had no genius for friendship with men . . .

'In the sunset of his great life, Lloyd George was left a lonely man. "The friendlessest man I ever knew," said one old Welsh follower of his.'

Ideally Frank Owen should have written *The Lloyd George I Knew* in a couple of hundred pages. He had worked as a researcher for the old Wizard, had been his follower, albeit briefly, in the Commons and interviewed him for Beaverbrook a number of times in the Hitler years. Now that would have been a good book!

In 1941, after a trip to see Lloyd George, Frank had told *Mirror* executive Cecil King that the old man had a 'mind like a scorpion'. Embittered by being characterised as another pessimistic Petain, Lloyd George accused Churchill of spending too much time 'looking down the barrels of guns' and making his speeches with one eye on the House of Commons and the other on posterity.

That finds no place in *Tempestuous Journey* which contains only the generalisation that Churchill's criticism had stung his fellow-statesman.

15. HUCKSTER OF DREAMS

Owen Glendower: I can call spirits from the
vasty deep. Hotspur: But will they come
when you do call for them?

Henry IV, Part I

RELEASED from his cavern of discontent, Frank Owen
took a new look at life. There was surely a better future
than stodgy hack work for a demanding taskmaster. In
February 1955 he resigned from the *Daily Express* and
made a world tour which took in Canada and Australia.
A series of new careers beckoned.

The first was a return to politics (see the next
chapter). Public relations looked a good option, commercial television was opening up and Frank had
contacts galore to set up a literary and serialisation
agency. All these purposes were combined in Frank
Owen Enterprises with Anna Phillips as Girl Friday and
steadying (she hoped) influence. 'My role as mistress
was of course all "in the shadows" ,' she explained.

Frank had begun on the commercial road in February
1953 with the founding of the Burma Star Club in
Hamilton Place, Park Lane. Field Marshal Bill Slim and
singer Vera Lynn were at the launch. The club was open
to the 6,000 members of the already-established Burma

Star Association of troops who had served in South East Asia Command.

'Frank's launching of the club was an extraordinary achievement,' said Anna. 'I've no idea how he managed it financially. The Park Lane location must have involved very heavy rent and rates. In comparison, prices and membership were minimal.'

The next venture, Frank Owen Enterprises, also had an impressive address: 10 Palace Chambers, Westminster, and stood opposite the Houses of Parliament. Anna recalls: 'In three years of business our only good PR account was with John King (now Lord King of British Airways fame). At that time he ran Pollard Ball Bearings with a small factory up North. We did his publicity and I remember Frank getting him an intro to Morgan Phillips, the secretary of the Labour Party. I knew John King of old. He had been Rodney's best man at our wedding.

'Frank had no business sense whatsoever and was always getting conned into lending his name to hair-brained schemes such as one to build a series of motels on main arterial roads. But it all came to nothing. Others with whom he had dealings included Peter Bessel (who appeared in the Jeremy Thorpe case) and Peter Baker MP, but there was very little substance in it all.'

Frank was rather more successful on the lecture and public speaking circuit. He was in demand at the Staff College, Camberley, and university debating unions, lectured at the London School of Economics and spoke at regimental dinners. His most important charitable activity was with the Saints and Sinners Club, whose secretary was an old *Daily Express* crony, crime correspondent Percy Hoskins. It included people from

Frank (left) at the first Remembrance Day Parade of Hereford's Burma Star Association

entertainment like Arthur Askey and Bud Flanagan, sportsmen Jack Solomons and Sir Stanley Rous and figures like Douglas Bader and Sir Malcolm Sargent. Frank Owen was chairman in 1960 and the dinner at the Dorchester that year was among his last public appearances of any note.

The opportunities provided by television quickly attracted Frank. He stood in for fellow-Herefordian Gilbert Harding (whom he heartily detested) in *What's My Line?* and presented a series of *Nine Days' Wonders* which dramatised such classic mysteries as the Marie Celeste. His most ambitious programme was *Personal Call*, where he visited and interviewed a celebrity. Subjects included Graham Sutherland, who had just painted a controversial portrait of Sir Winston Churchill, and Sir Bernard Docker, the BSA motor cycle magnate whose flamboyant wife was a frequent subject of 1950s headlines. Sir Bernard and Frank swam quite happily in the Docker pool during the programme but the millionaire's shrill wife was not happy about something said.

TV critics panned Frank as too pugnacious an interviewer. (He was obviously in the business before his time). He had joined Associated Rediffusion in the middle of 1955 as a news commentator. A year later, as the Suez Crisis was building up, he was sent to the Middle East and produced a notable exclusive. This was a filmed interview with Gamel Abdel Nasser, the Egyptian president who had just nationalised the Suez Canal and was to withstand the Anglo-French-Israeli invasion which would lead to the fall of Anthony Eden. The interview was much praised. Then, remarkably, perhaps alcoholically, Frank Owen's television career fizzled out.

Few newspaper features were more eagerly read in the 1950s than memoirs of the recently ended war. A smalltime crook called Eddie Chapman had such a tale to tell, Frank Owen undertook to market it and editor Reg Cudlipp bought it to serialise in the *News of the World*.

The former safebreaker claimed he had been a successful double agent. Captured in the Channel Islands, Chapman apparently persuaded his German captors to send him as a spy to Britain where he resumed his native loyalty and worked against the Nazis. Cudlipp recalled: 'I publicised the story with a front page splash. But while the early editions were rolling, some "kind friend" on another paper drew the story to the attention of an Admiral Thomson, then in charge of "D" Notices (which warned the Press off certain sensitive items).

'Thomson telephoned me saying the memoirs had not been cleared by the War Office – which contradicted what Frank had told me and fully believed! I had to drop the splash announcement from later editions, notably that sold in London. This upset Frank when his papers were delivered next morning.

'We lived in blocks of flats opposite each other. When he saw me emerge from the front door of Marsham Court he bellowed from the seventh floor of Westminster Gardens: "What happened to the puff for the spy story?"

"They stopped it."

"They can't bloody well do that."

"But, Frank, they have!"

'I was summoned to MI5 at the War Office on the Monday morning. They waffled on about the Russians learning our secrets. I told them what happened during the war could be of no interest to the Russians now. They replied: "Intelligence methods are never out of date. We still use some ideas from the Napoleonic Wars," to which I could only retort: "No wonder the last war lasted so long." '

To retrieve his investment Reg Cudlipp got permission to publish an edited version which read as if it were about a single not a double spy. In 1956 Frank managed to get the complete story published as a book.

That was not the end of the Eddie Chapman saga. It finished up as a film called *Triple Cross* in 1967 with Christopher Plummer, Yul Brynner and Trevor Howard. In the hands of director Terence Young (*Dr No* and *From Russia With Love*), it became a James Bond-style romp and lost whatever little credence it originally had. One hopes at least that it provided Frank Owen with some royalties in his time of dire need.

A second potboiler hit the bookstalls in 1957. This was about the Argentine dictator, Peron, his rise and fall. Anna Phillips described how Frank got involved with a scar-faced Canadian former air pilot called Paul Brewster who had an 'in' to the Peron family. Frank went out to Argentina for additional material. 'In the meantime,' said Anna, 'I had driven out to Spain in Frank's brand new Jaguar with a chap called David Thomson, who also had South American connections.

'Frank was due to fly back from Buenos Aires and pick me and the Jag up in Madrid but he never showed. I returned by plane and I suppose the Jag was driven back by someone. That was Frank all over.'

The last Owen book was *The Fall of Singapore*, which was the copyright of Beaverbrook Newspapers (still looking after their prodigal son who also remained in his company flat). The book, which went from hard-back to three paperback printings, was a competent job and well-illustrated but said nothing new about the 1942 campaign in which the Japanese gobbled up Malaya.

16. LAST HURRAH

Hereford's son, second to none —
Election chant

A tip from the top of the Senior Service enticed Frank Owen back into politics. He met Mountbatten, who was between commanding the Mediterranean Fleet and becoming First Sea Lord, the Royal Navy's professional head, in 1955. The admiral's political chief, known as the First Lord of the Admiralty, was J P L (Jimmy) Thomas, Hereford's MP since he won the seat off Frank 24 years previously.

Mountbatten confided in Frank that Thomas would fight the 1955 General Election but was likely to retire from office into the Lords in the middle of the next Parliament. If Frank fought the constituency and came a respectable second, he would have a good chance of knocking out a new Tory candidate in the by-election.

In the January he got himself co-opted on to the Liberal Party Council along with John Arlott, Nancy Seear and Jeremy Thorpe. Just before the May election he breezed into Hereford, where the party was moribund, having failed to field a candidate in 1951. He offered to stand, paying his own expenses, and brought a little entourage including Ronnie Cornwell, one of his flashy friends from London. While Frank stayed modestly at his father's old pub, the Black Swan, Cornwell (father of thriller writer John Le Carre) was in the city's top hotel, the Green Dragon.

It was a brief campaign, starting with Frank riding the top of a taxi in the Hightown. Liberal leader Clement Davies spoke at an eve-of-poll rally which attracted 2,000 locals who had not forgotten the 'boy MP'. He travelled the constituency in style in his Jaguar XJ140 drophead coupe and once again impressed the citizens with his forceful delivery and good looks.

It was good showing against such an established MP, whom Frank called 'the admiral of the River Wye'. The final figures were:

J P L Thomas (Con)	18,058
F Owen (Lib)	 8,658
Mrs P Seers (Lab)	 8,154
Majority	 9,400

So far the gamble was good. The Liberals had edged into second place. That was the dummy run.

Now the pay-off. Less than a year later Jimmy Thomas became Lord Cilcennin and Frank was ready for the February 1956 by-election. Snow and ice beset the campaign. On polling day Frank cut his nose in a skid on a frozen road near Ross-on-Wye. He was not the only Owen casualty. Grace campaigned with three broken fingers, an injury caused when Jojo the poodle snagged his lead in a car door. That made headlines, as did the arrival of cabaret performer Frances Day to boost the Liberal cause.

The party's top showman was Count Dominic De

The candidate — note face plasters after car crash

Foe, one of the early TV personalities and a magician. At the adoption meeting in the Shire Hall, De Foe drummed up £340 in an instant fighting fund appeal but, to Frank's chagrin, organised an eve-of-the poll torchlight procession which cost the candidate £200 'out of my pocket'.

Future Liberal leaders Jo Grimond and Jeremy Thorpe spoke for the candidate. Thorpe recalled more than 30 years later: 'It was extraordinary how Frank got better and better as the campaign progressed and at the end became the old sparkling candidate who had originally won the seat. One of his quips about the Tory Prime Minister was: "Sir Anthony Eden is as much good as a poultice on a wooden leg." He generated a lot of enthusiasm and at his final torchlight rally I can remember the crowds chanting: "Hereford's son! Second to none!"

At a score of venues the Basingstoke burr of John Arlott − so familiar to cricket fans − boosted the cause. John and Frank were old drinking mates from their days with the Harmsworth papers, meeting regularly in the nearby pocket-handkerchief pub, Auntie's. Frank, as *Daily Mail* editor, had once despatched John, a part-time *Evening News* columnist, to cover Harold Larwood's 1950 emigration to Australia from Tilbury Docks. Arlott was the only reporter present for this evocative occasion and produced an exclusive for the *Mail*. They were still rare cronies and disagreed only about their tipple − Frank preferred Scotch, John was a wine connoisseur.

Another supporter was Peter Bessel, who increased the Liberal vote at the recent Torquay by-election and was to achieve national prominence in the

1979 trial of Jeremy Thorpe. Frank Owen had business dealings with Bessel in the 1950s but quarrelled with him over money, said Anna Phillips.

Frank's 'harem' was out in force, not only Grace but also sister Marjorie, Lady Jackson from Upton Bishop and Frances Day. There was almost another. Photojournalist Derek Evans, a Young Liberal at that time, described the panic when local party headquarters heard that Anna Phillips was on her way to Hereford while Grace was there at her husband's side. Evans was one of two party workers deputised to 'head Anna off at the pass'. They met the London train and persuaded the lady to make an immediate return journey. She was not amused.

The Owen camp pulled out all the stops. Messages of support – some doubtless solicited – rolled in to dazzle the electors. From *SEAC* days Field Marshal Auchinleck, General Sir Montague Stopford and Vera Lynn, wartime Air Marshals Sir Keith Park and Pathfinder Bennett, cricketer C B Fry, boxing promoter Jack Solomons, authors J B Priestley, A P Herbert, Compton Mackenzie and Neville Cardus, actor Jack Hawkins, they all rallied round.

Doug Hughes, one of the Liberals' most enthusiastic workers, recalled the traditional hustings on a Saturday night – after the pubs had closed – with Frank revelling in the cut-and-thrust of argument and throw-

On pages following:
John Arlott speaks at a 1956 Election Rally in
Hereford Cattle Market, flanked by Frank whose
'harem' (l. to r.) sister
Marjorie, Lady Jackson, and wife Grace, are
prominent in the front

Young Liberals' eve-of-poll torchlight rally 1956

ing the jibes of hecklers back into their teeth with powerful barbs of his own. 'That was real politics,' Hughes said.

After all that, the Liberal gamble failed by only 2,000 or so as the 'Galloping Major', David Gibson-Watt MC (and two bars), kept the Tory flag flying:

D Gibson-Watt (Con)	12,124
F Owen (Lib)	 9,979
B Stanley (Lab)	 5,277
Majority	 2,150

This was the last Owen hurrah in Hereford. Frank's father, Tommy, still survived at 79 and his mother, Cicely, was 73, never now to see their masterful son back in Parliament.

Arlott, who twice fought Epping for the Liberals, maintained his political double act with Frank. Another leading Liberal, Lord (Emlyn) Hooson, recalls an encounter with the pair at a later 1956 by-election: 'I was in practice as a barrister on the Wales and Chester Circuit and we had a house on the Chester city walls. Frank Owen and John Arlott stayed with us after speaking for the candidate. We stayed up most of the night chatting about various things. During the course of that night Frank consumed a whole bottle of whisky (which none of the rest of us drank) and, even more surprisingly, Arlott drank a whole bottle of Celebration Cream sherry.'

In 1958 Frank Owen quit as Hereford prospective candidate (to be succeeded by TV's Robin Day) and also

On pages following:
The Victory that never was . . .

143

HEREFORD
ELECTION NEWS

Passing thro' 14th February, 1956 · "FOR THOSE WHO DARE TO THINK" · Complimentary.

FRANK OWEN POISED FOR VICTORY!

Local Man People's Choice

In dramatic fashion FRANK OWEN, O.B.E., the Liberal Candidate for Hereford has galvanised the By-Election. With his drive, energy and forthright speaking he has made a profound impression on those members of the constituency that hadn't already met this dynamic candidate. And as the canvass returns pour into the Liberal Fighting H.Q. at the Liberal Club, Election Agent Edward Dunford is able to report a rising tide of enthusiasm for someone who is, admittedly, the only LOCAL candidate in the fight. It is clear that many Labour voters have realised that, with their candidate bottom last time they can have no hope of success, and that to keep the Tory out, every anti-Conservative vote must come to FRANK OWEN who is the real challenger. On the other side, many former Tory voters have announced their intentions of supporting FRANK OWEN, if only because of the threat of the economic situation, which FRANK OWEN predicted with such deadly accuracy at the last election. And so, with an ever increasing round of activity and a whirlwind last-minute round up of every vote, FRANK OWEN completes the campaign that looks very much as if it will again return him to Westminster. Be assured that only a wastage of pro-Owen votes can keep him out, and it is therefore IMPERATIVE that **every supporter of FRANK OWEN POLLS FOR HIM** on the 14th of February. And one last word—there is a limit to the number of cars that can be used at a by-election, so it would be a tremendous help if all Owen supporters would make their own way to the poll. BUT VOTE, AND MAKE A CHANCE OF TRIUMPH A CERTAINTY. On the 14th, VOTE HEREFORD'S SON SECOND TO NONE.

ONLY VOTES FOR THE LABOUR CANDIDATE CAN PUT THE TORY IN

VOTE HEREFORD'S SON
SECOND TO NONE

TUESDAY, FEBRUARY 14th

FRANK OWEN SPEAKS OUT

Tories Fail to Help Countryman

"WHEN ELECTED I SHALL PRESS FOR ROSS INDUSTRIES"

Dramatic Promise of Help

As the campaign fought so brilliantly by Frank Owen has gone on, Frank Owen (the only local candidate) has become steadily more indignant at what he has characterised as "The callous neglect of our countryfolk over the years ". In a speech at Ross he said : " I am certain that thousands of pounds are spent each year by those from Ross who have to go each day to seek work out of the area. That money is Ross money and should be spent there, too. If I am trusted with the votes of the people and am returned, I shall press in every way for added industries to be brought to Ross to stop the wicked drain of Ross labour out of the town."

On the question of electricity and water, Frank Owen is equally caustic : " Of course industry lags, when the vital power is lacking—and not only industry suffers from this—but the hundreds of householders who year after year are having to endure sub-standard lighting because of the failure of BOTH THE MAIN PARTIES to bring power to their areas. It isn't a case of money," he declared, " the money is found year after year to cover losses on national-ised industries, it MUST be found for these vital tasks—it will pay a rich dividend in the long run."

Asked about Education, Frank Owen again made no apologies for his downright approach. " I hear of too many stories of children have to travel as many as 38 miles a day to reach schools nearer the towns. This is grossly unfair and I shall press hard for a more just arrangement that will not continually put the country child at a disadvantage. I shall also press for more equitable distribution of Grammar School places—so that the allocation will depend more frequently on ability rather than the number of places a particular area has available."

Finally, Frank Owen said : " I am sure my friends in the town will join with me in this campaign to bring justice to the glorious countryside of Hereford. There is so much that even a single member can accomplish, that I hope that all will vote for me on the 14th, and by so doing bring more happiness to all our voters, and a fuller life for all our Herefordians."

READ AND JUDGE !
Is there a Better Candidate ?

145

★ SUPPORT THE MAN WITH A POLICY FOR THE PEOPLE ★

FRANK OWEN'S PARENTS TAKE A HAND

For the third time Mr. & Mrs. Owen, well-known local figures, and parents of the Liberal candidate Frank Owen, are taking an active part in the whirlwind campaign of their son.

Although Mr. T. H. Owen is 79, it hasn't prevented him giving much trenchant advice on the conduct of the campaign, and Mrs. Owen who is 73 has been very busy calling up supporters, providing rosettes and generally speeding the way to victory. Miss M. Owen (Frank Owen's sister) has also arrived to assist in the vital duty of getting the thousands of Owen supporters to the Poll on the 14th. Everywhere there is confidence that this noted local family will again have a son a member at Westminster. And all Hereford is saying : "**Vote HEREFORD'S son Second to None**".

FRANK OWEN, O.B.E., has had tremendous meetings throughout the constituency. At the Cattle Market, in High Town, and throughout the villages, large and enthusiastic meetings have acclaimed the words of the only Hereford candidate in the fight. His fighting utterances have made a great impact.

POINT OF VIEW !

Canvasser : "Good morning, madam. I've called on behalf of Frank Owen the Liberal. I hope you are going to vote for him?"

Householder : "Oh, no, I'm voting Labour, not for those awful socialists!"

OLDEST LIBERAL WORKS FOR FRANK OWEN

Among the keenest supporters of Frank Owen must be numbered Mr. Daniel O'Neil, a man who although confined to a wheel chair and in his 89th year has been a loyal worker in the most active sense of the word. His hard work is an inspiration to all

When young Tory hecklers were busy interrupting a Liberal meeting they were finally silenced by a very old lady (who declined to give her name) who said "You shut up, Frank Owen has done more for us when he was in than any Tory ever has."

FRANK OWEN — THE MAN LOYAL TO HEREFORD

FRANK OWEN has a record unequalled by his opponents in this fight.

He has NEVER CONTESTED ANY OTHER SEAT THAN HEREFORD, and he doesn't intend to look elsewhere for a way to Parliament ; if he is to be an M.P. it will be only on the vote of his own folk. It should be noted that the Tory has twice been defeated in another area, and that the Labour candidate has been specially " imported " to make a fight of it. Vote for Loyalty. VOTE FOR OWEN.

THE NATIONAL PRESS WATCH FRANK OWEN

Observers from all the National press have been watching this vital campaign—drawn here only through the fame of Frank Owen.

Frank Owen (himself a former newspaper editor) has also been invited to contribute a daily article in one of the big national dailies. This only shows the importance of the result, and Frank Owen is the one candidate that can capture the national headlines when he is returned.

THE NATION NEEDS FRANK OWEN and Hereford is the constituency that is able to return him.

VOTE FOR OWEN, the candidate who really MATTERS. He is the man that knows the Job—BECAUSE HE HAS DONE IT BEFORE.

LAST WORD

In this paper we have tried to show the Liberal point of view. Ask yourself these questions :

Apart from FRANK OWEN, is there another candidate who :

Is a national figure in his own right ?

Has held the seat before ?

Is the only challenger to the Tories ?

Has had an unequalled record in his career ?

Who as a member has already shown that he is a first class member (see page 1) ?

If there is NO OTHER—VOTE OWEN.

LIBERALS RALLY TO ACHIEVE VICTORY

LIBERALS from all parts of Britain have come to join in Frank Owen's victory campaign. Amongst the speakers who have visited the area include JOSEPH GRIMOND, M.P., the Chief Liberal Whip, MR. JOHN ARLOTT, the well-known broadcaster ; MR. JEREMY THORPE, the prospective Candidate for South Devon ; MR. EDWIN MALLINDINE, the Candidate for North Cornwall (who came within 1,500 votes of victory) ; MR. PETER BESSELL, the candidate from the Torquay by-election, who was the only candidate there to increase his vote ; MR. DOMINIC LE FOE, the TV performer, also has spoken at numerous meetings in the constituency.

Teams of canvassers from adjoining areas have also visited the fight, and donations of money have been made from all over Britain.

At the Frank Owen Adoption meeting over £340 was subscribed by members of the local association—and over 500 people attended in contrast to the low attendances of his opponents' meetings. Success is in the air !

The Call to Youth

One of the most inspiring features of the campaign has been the rally of young people to Frank Owen's cause. Teams of keen and intelligent young people have been out night after night on the doorsteps of the city and villages carrying Frank Owen's message to the electors.

It is only natural that such a vigorous candidate as Frank Owen should attract such keen youth, for the Liberal policy is essentially one of youthful energy. Thus it is, that a great party with a mature candidate has also attracted the vigorous and thinking people of a more recent generation.

JUSTICE FOR THE OLD AGE PENSIONERS

LIBERALS, who pioneered [Old Age Pensions (the Liberal Government of 1906, in face of tremendous Tory opposition introduced the measure) say that to-day it is essential that pensions both for the old and the war pensioners, should be pegged to the cost of living. This is the only way to achieve justice for those who no longer work. Liberals (and that is Frank Owen, too !) also say that if an Old Age Pensioner can earn a few shillings it is only just that he should have them and that it shouldn't be deducted from his pension. After all, retired officers may take jobs.

MRS. OWEN PLAYS HER PART

SEVENTEENTH WEDDING ANNIVERSARY

Among Frank Owen's legion of helpers has been his attractive American born wife Grace. She has played no little part in the campaign, and has been a familiar figure at the numerous meetings which he has addressed throughout his hectic campaign. An added joy in the middle of the heat of battle has been the celebration of their SEVENTEENTH wedding anniversary, which was duly celebrated with gifts of flowers and chocolates ! Among Mrs. Owen's special interests, are Anglo-American relations, the care of the Old Age Pensioners, and child welfare. In a message to electors she says : " I hope very much that you will all vote for my husband. I know that he is a stalwart fighter for the things in which he believes. I know, too, that he is keenly devoted to the family unit in the British way of life."

Printed by Jakemans Ltd., 31 Church St., Hereford, and published by Edward Dunford, Agent, Liberal Club, Widemarsh Street, Hereford. 10/2/56.

FRANK QUOTES

" Even Anthony Eden has noticed our troubles now—dear old Anthony the Unready ".

* * *

" If the Tories knew there was a crisis coming—then they were rogues—if they didn't know they were fools. Take your choice."

* * *

" I don't see why you should be asked to accept someone that Brecon & Radnor have twice declined."

* * *

" The Tories have turned the Empire into an Imperial slum."

* * *

" We've already had the Butler Squeeze, now you had better prepare for the Macmillan hug."

147

resigned as chairman of the party's national publicity committee. Four years later he appeared on the Liberal short list for a Monmouthshire seat. Then in 1974 there was a bizarre attempt to get him to fight Hereford for the fifth time – as an anti-Thorpe Liberal at the age of 69.

When he ceased to be candidate Frank's public appearances in Hereford were confined to functions of the local Burma Star branch of which he was a founder member. He stayed at his father's old pub, the Black Swan, with George Farmer, the licensee, who had met him as an airman in Burma. Frank and Grace were honoured guests of George and his wife, Lina, both there and at their next Hereford hotel, the Arden. 'One remarkable thing Frank could do,' said George. 'He could be rapidly writing a letter or article while holding a conversation with you on a totally different matter. Never known anybody else who could do that.'

The Burma Star Association was Frank's last great loyalty. He was the founding editor of its national magazine, *Dekho*, and helped start the Hereford branch, marching with his comrades on Remembrance Day and attending other local functions. At the annual Burma Star reunions in the Royal Albert Hall he always met the Hereford contingent at a particular bar.

* * * * * *

Came the 1960s and the Owen firebrand began showing signs of burn-out. In 1960 Anna Phillips 'broke off our liaison in despair at the deterioration in Frank's personality and a sense of a dead end for myself'. She emigrated to the States but stayed there only a couple of years.

Beaverbrook died in 1964 and Frank was bereft of the patron who pensioned and housed him. Four years later his wife, Grace, died.

During the 70s Frank's name emerged from time to time. In March 1973 Michael Foot threw a House of Commons dinner in Frank's honour attended by Jenny Lee, Tom Driberg and current *Standard* editor Charles Wintour, and in 1975 the Press Club gave him a 70th birthday lunch.

Sometime in this period he called at Anna's home in Camden Town unannounced. 'He was a broken, lonely and broke old man,' she said. 'His clothes were threadbare.'

Another encounter was with a Mrs Carol Matthews who recalled: 'We were keeping the Somerville Hotel in Bodenham Road, Hereford. It had been Wolferlow, the home of the Owen family. Towards the late 1970s Frank Owen came to our door and asked if he could look over the home of his childhood. When we took him out to the summer-house, he said: 'This is where we used to change for tennis.' He was happy to see the house so well kept. He was rather emotional and had the glazed look of an old, beaten man. It was a startling contrast from the dynamic orator I had listened to in the elections 20 years earlier.'

Frank Owen OBE, MA (Cantab), Freeman of the City of London, Saint and Sinner, died in a Worthing nursing home on January 23, 1979. 'This is the way the world ends. Not with a bang but a whimper.'

Toasts

THE LOYAL TOAST

OUR GUESTS

Proposed by   Lord Evans, G.C.V.O., M.D., F.R.C.P.

Response by   The Rt. Hon. Lord Brabazon of Tara,
                                                    G.B.E., LL.D.

THE PRESERVATION OF THE "SAINTS"

Proposed by   Sir Alan Herbert

Response by   The Rt. Hon. Lord Birkett, Q.C.

THE "SAINTS AND SINNERS CLUB" OF LONDON

Proposed by   The Marquess of Exeter, K.C.M.G.

Response by   The Chairman,
                                Frank Owen, Esq., O.B.E.

Incidental Music

by the

Sidney Jerome Orchestra

At the conclusion of his speech, Mr. Owen will formally hand over the Chair to his successor, Sir Ronald Howe, C.V.O., M.C.

The Toast list for saint and sinner Frank

The old boy . . .

POSTSCRIPT: THE MAX FACTOR

Beaverbrook had an intentionally
demoralising effect on his young men
Sir Stafford Cripps

SOME Liberals saw Frank Owen as lost leader, seduced from his true destiny as the result of the riches and patronage lavished on him by the evil Beaverbrook. One who favoured this theory was Clement Davies, leader of the party from 1945 to 1956. 'We lost the power of his oratory and the incisiveness of his young mind at a time the party could ill afford to do so,' Davies told Grenville Jones who fought Leominster for the party in the 1950s.

But who was Clem Davies to make this comment? He started in Parliament at the same time as Frank Owen, having been elected for Montgomery in 1929. When, a couple of years later, Frank remained faithful to Lloyd George and lost his Hereford seat to a National Government Tory, Clem Davies became a National Liberal which meant he was re-elected on a pact, facing no Conservative opponent.

The Davies record in the 1930s was that of an appeaser. He became a member of the Anglo-German Fellowship which included many right wing Tories with Nazi sympathies and included Reich Foreign Minister

Ribbentrop on its guest list.

His Parliamentary record was interesting. In December 1935 Davies was among those who opposed a motion condemning the Hoare-Laval Pact as calculated to reward Italy, the declared aggressor, at the expense of Abyssinia, the victim, and destroy collective security.

The following year Davies opposed an amendment to the address by a member of his own party to establish a Ministry of Supply to organise armaments against the dictators. Then in October, 1938, the Member for Montgomery voted in the Munich debate to support Chamberlain's policy. He did eventually distance himself from the Anglo-German Fellowship and voted against Chamberlain in the May, 1940 debate that led to the Prime Minister's downfall. But by then, there were many conversions on the road to Dunkirk.

When Clem Davies arrived to address the Hereford candidate's eve-of-poll rally in 1955, Frank Owen made the wry comment: 'Somebody ought to ask him about what he did in 1931.'

But other people made the point about the way the charismatic radical had been lured to Fleet Street. Beaverbrook was frequently his own recruiting sergeant. In 1932, for instance, campaigning on his Empire platform, he travelled north to address a meeting at Darwen. *The Manchester Guardian* sent a seasoned but obscure 42-year-old reporter to cover the meeting: Howard Spring. As he walked through the local Saturday market Spring was intrigued by the persuasive, hard-sell stallholders and hucksters. He was reminded of them as he listened to Beaverbrook whom he called a 'pedlar of dreams'.

The *Guardian* sub-editor lifted the phrase to headline

the report, Beaverbrook read it and instantly hired Spring. This was no dynamic political writer, his lordship soon discovered and sent him to be the *Evening Standard*'s book reviewer. This set the direction of Spring's rise to fame. Late in life he joined the ranks of best-selling novelists with such titles as *Shabby Tiger* and *Fame is the Spur.*

Another 'personal signing' was that of rugby international forward Peter Howard, who wrote years later: 'As a young man I was married and poor. A friend of mine who worked on the *Express* took me . . . to the Empire Crusade Club. People there spoke about Empire Free Trade . . . All seemed to favour it. Some were fatuous. I rose to my feet and said so.'

To Howard's astonishment he was approached by Beaverbrook, 'a short, vigorous man whose head seemed too heavy for his body', who shook his hand and saw to it that Howard's views were printed in the next afternoon's *Standard.* Two weeks later Beaverbrook sent for Howard and said: 'I hear you are going to write a political article for me.' This was the start of 'seven rich years (during which) I sat at his feet and wrote articles on politics, the Empire, tobacco, pubs and every subject on earth.'

We have already seen how Beaverbrook invited the youthful left wing writer, Michael Foot, to join him at Cherkley, asked him to summarise that day's newspapers and instantly put him on the payroll. There seems no record of how Frank Owen was recruited several years earlier but, as a maverick ex-MP with a high profile, there seems little doubt he was one of the proprietor's personal appointees.

Frank was highly paid from the start. Eventually as

editor of the *Standard* he was on £4,000 a year, equal perhaps to £80,000 or £100,000 in 1990s terms. Beaverbrook supplemented his Army pay handsomely, lost him for a few post-war years to the *Daily Mail* but took him back on the books to write features for the *Express* and work on the Lloyd George biography. Through all the twists and turns of Frank's later life he was a Beaverbrook pensioner, including the tenure of an expensive Central London flat . . . until his patron died.

After his 1931 election defeat Frank Owen twice turned down a political comeback. First, soon after the Patsy scandal, he resigned as Hereford prospective candidate. Even without the embarrassment of his mistress's death, it seems likely he would have chosen to stay in the dynamic world of Fleet Street. He said in a 1937 interview: 'I am glad I went through the House of Commons but even happier I got it out of my system before I was 25.'

Then in 1945 he resisted several approaches to join the Labour Party list of candidates, so missing the great Attlee landslide. At the time, however, Frank was absorbed in his *SEAC* crusade and believed he had a glowing future ahead on Rothermere's *Daily Mail.*

When he did at last turn back to politics he failed narrowly. As Jeremy Thorpe remarked: 'Frank very nearly won in 1956. How he would have fared in his reincarnation as an MP I cannot say. Success would largely turn on how rigorously Frank avoided the all-too-many bars in the House.'

Geoffrey Cox, a pre-war *Express* foreign correspondent wrote that but for Beaverbrook Frank Owen might have joined Labour and 'taken his place alongside

Gaitskell, and Evan Durbin, Douglas Jay and Hector McNeil as a minister in the post-war Labour Government instead of ending his days as a hard-drinking literary pensioner of Beaverbrook.'

Cox concluded: 'Owen was not the first or the last Fleet Street figure to regard alcohol and journalism as natural partners and he did, after all edit with distinction two Fleet Street newspapers.'

On balance, I think he gave more to journalism that he ever would have contributed to politics and government.

APPENDIX I:

FRANK OWEN (1905 – 79)

Nov 4	1905	Born in Hereford
Autumn	1916	Starts at Monmouth School
Autumn	1923	Goes up to Cambridge
Summer	1927	First class honours
	1927	Joins S. Wales Argus
May 1	1929	Elected MP for Hereford
Oct 27	1931	Loses Hereford
	1932	Joins *Daily Express*
Aug	1938	Edits *Evening Standard*
Feb 4	1939	Marries Grace McGillivray
Mar 26	1942	Called up to RAC
Dec 20	1943	Commissioned
Jan 10	1944	Launches *SEAC*
July 4	1946	Joins *Daily Mail*
Mar 4	1947	Editor, *Daily Mail*
May 25	1950	Quits *Daily Mail*
May 26	1955	Loses Hereford general election
Feb 4	1956	Loses Hereford by-election
Oct 31	1968	Grace Owen dies
Jan 23	1979	Frank Owen dies

APPENDIX II:

A HOMELY PARLIAMENT — My first day in the House
[By Frank Owen, the youngest MP in the House]

THERE was a conspiracy of things yesterday to tune affairs exactly to the quiet advent of a Labour Parliament to Westminster.

I had never seen Parliament opened, nor even been in the House of Commons until I entered it to take the oath as Member.

But I treasured visions of solemn pageantry, of Kings and Lords and Commons, of gold and scarlet and ermine, of the peeresses like goddesses on their high gallery gazing down with Olympian grace upon the panoply of history below, of coaches of state and horses and men gaily caparisoned to do honour to the King and to his faithful Commons when he comes to speak to them across the floor of the House of Peers.

Yesterday no sun shone for Members as they hurried into the House. There were no trumpets and there was no King. The only colour was the modest blue and brown of our ladies.

Black Rod appears at the Bar of the House and desires the attendance of Mr Speaker and the Commons in another place to hear the King's Speech read by his Commission. When the King comes, he does not desire, but commands attendance.

In their own House the Commons hear the Speech read to them again. It exactly reflects the outlook and the temper of the Labour Parliament. The speeches are in the same strain — one delightful and non-contentious, the rest non-contentious. The ex-Prime Minister pleads for a united House; the new Prime Minister hopes everyone will co-operate with him. Mr Winston Churchill sits silent until the Labour benches roar: 'Smile, Winnie.' He is probably thinking he could impart a little liveliness to the proceedings if he had the chance.

Parliament was altogether too homely to be impressive to a stranger. Fortunately 615 in a family leaves scope for those domestic differences which make home the most exciting place in the world.

Daily News, July 3 1929

APPENDIX III:

BLITZKRIEG

(From *Guilty Men* and containing Frank Owen's analysis of Hitler's strategy).

WHEN Hitler was threatening Czechoslovakia in September, 1938, Dr. Edouard Beneš, President of the country, apprised the British Government of the following information: Germany has five armoured divisions and Czechoslovakia has four. No notice was taken of this information.

I here raise in precise form the question I have asked in general terms in an earlier chapter: Was this statement put before the Staffs of the French and not the British armies? If it was, who rejected it? If it was not, why was it not?

On May 10, 1940, Hitler struck in the West with *blitzkrieg* fury. Head and front of the German onslaught were nine armoured divisions co-operating with innumerable airplane squadrons that consigned to the dustbin the assurances of Messrs. Baldwin, Chamberlain, Hoare and Kingsley Wood that we were either getting or had got 'air parity'.

The *blitzkrieg*. It means lightning-war . . . Hitler's onslaught was delivered in six waves against Holland and Belgium. The main strategy which directed the invasions was that which had so brilliantly served 'Politicissimo' Hitler. Divide and Conquer. Divide and conquer Liberals, Socialists, Communists, Catholics, Conservatives. Divide and conquer Austrians, Czechs, England and France. The German armies thrust between the Dutch and the Belgians. The rest of the operation was to envelop the weaker army and compel its annihilation or surrender.

The military instrument Hitler employed was a completely merged and perfectly synchronised use of (a) motorised advance guard, (b) airplanes-cum-tanks, (c) motorised infantry-cum-artillery, (d) Fifth column treachery.

These tactics have been described as 'revolutionary'. This word conceals the surprise and the dismay with which our rulers faced them. In sober fact these tactics were derived and developed from the last war which Britain carried to a victorious conclusion in 1918.

In 1940 the newspapers suddenly became filled with discussion and explanation of the operation called 'infiltration'. Hitler's armoured divisions had thrown themselves suddenly and violently against the Allied positions and either by crossing yielded bridgeheads along the Albert Canal (Belgian) and the Meuse River (French) or by expeditious and efficient pontooning had passed the river barriers and were 'fanning-out' behind the Allied lines.

The tanks charged on – to Arras, Amiens, Abbeville, eventually to Boulogne and Calais. In none of these places did they encounter serious initial resistance – though later a hastily gathered garrison of battalions from the Rifle Brigade, 60th Rifles, Queen Victoria Rifles and the Tank Corps, in all 4,000 men, were flung into the citadel of Calais to cover the Dunkirk evacuation. They held it four days, and as far as we know thirty wounded men fell into the enemy hands alive.

At Arras German motor-cyclist troops swept into the

town with Tommy guns on their handle bars and seized the key points in a few hours. There were no line-of-communication troops to oppose them, and the railway station was eventually regained for a day or two by Sappers and Royal Army Service Corps armed with rifle and bayonet. At Abbeville, fifty miles behind 'the front', the stationmaster was chatting to a British officer on leave when the German motor-cyclists rode up and relieved him of his duties.

But really there was nothing 'revolutionary' in all this. In 1915 the intelligent French Infantry captain, André Laffargue, had already discerned the principle of 'infiltration' which simply means that when your attack is held up by a few strong points you pass around and beyond them, like a tide washing against rocks. It was the Germans who first employed this (then really revolutionary) idea to the full. In March, 1918, their infantry waves poured through the Allied defences. *All that Hitler has done is to speed up the tides.*

Hitler has put the first wave of infantrymen on motor-cycles. He has given them, in the shape of tanks, a mechanised ram to smash in the enemy front. Instead of the old barrage of shells from more or less stationary field batteries, Hitler has given his attack troops flying artillery which covers their advance with a curtain of bombs. This artillery lacks the immense weight of the heavy bombardment and barrage which preceded and accompanied the infantry assaults of 1915-18. It makes up for this deficiency by its sheer 'terrifying' power against troops − at least at first − and of course by its mobility. Thus when the tanks are held up they do not have to report back to artillery Headquarters. The air artillery can see the check for themselves. All they have to do is to go and get some more bombs.

These tactics had been thoroughly discussed for many years past and the mechanisation and motorisation of the British Army had been urged notably by the new Chief of Imperial General Staff, General Sir John Dill, by Major General Wavell and Major General Fuller.

The mechanisers were not turned down. The War Office, that is the responsible Government, adopted the Baldwin technique towards this problem which required firm and immediate handling. They accepted mechanisation in principle. The survivors of Dunkirk know what the politicians did in practice.

During the Spanish Civil War, in the battle of the Ebro of 1937, we witnessed the first actual tests of this tank-airplane-motorised infantry. The brave Republican infantry and field artillery simply melted before it. Those who presented these facts to leading politicians in the Government were smiled on with pity and patronisingly told 'But these Republican militiamen were only a rabble'.

In Poland even the British Government had to notice the military conduct of its ally. It had to observe the German Army deploy its strength *and its tactics*. These were the tactics of the Ebro, multiplied indeed and diversified. The German armoured columns thrust deep salients into the Polish lines. In vain the Polish cavalry sought to strike against them. The German airplanes detected the Polish concentration and destroyed it. The German flanks were guarded by the German skies. (The Polish Air Force had been obliterated on the ground during the first day.)

The German tanks galloped across the Polish plain and entered Warsaw within ten days. They were driven out, but kept cruising around. In eighteen days the Polish Army was smashed. In London the same men who had made a military alliance with a cavalry army that they could not reach even by sea to reinforce shook their heads and said 'What can you expect from Poles?'

What is the answer to the mechanised and motorised army? The first answer, and in the end the final answer, is — another mechanised army. But pending the building of that army of counter-blow what can we do?

The answer is defence-in-depth, which means the abandonment of the archaic idea of 'lines' of defence and the adoption of the idea of 'zones'. This is the tactic whereby you yield the outpost line in order to contest the enemy in the main battle zone or even in the rearward battle zone. This, too, is not 'revolutionary'. It was all worked out by Colonel von Lossberg in the last war, and by him put to deadly use in the building of the Hindenburg Line in 1916. This tactic of elastic defence has been studied by the British Army for twenty years and young officers in 1939 were lectured on it. But was it employed in the British Zone in Flanders?

Of course the so-called Gort Line had *some* depth. The kind of depth which would have enabled it to stand the infantry assaults of 1918. Unhappily the assaults of 1940 were mechanised.

It is true that the 'Gort Line' was never penetrated. It was turned. The French on the right flank let the Germans into 'The Bulge'. The B.E.F. fell back in orderly retreat from their prepared positions. But the Germans had completely destroyed our rear. Indeed they occupied it. No more shells, supplies or reinforcements could get up to the Army, the Germans were even intercepting the letters to our troops.

The Germans did not cut the B.E.F. off from its communications. They cut off communications from the B.E.F. In fact, the Germans encountered no defence-in-depth. Behind the British Army, either when it had advanced to the line of the Dyle in Belgium itself or when it had retired beyond the Gort Line on the frontier there was no defended 'zone'. Nor was there any adequate mobile reserve.

But why was there no adequate mobile reserve? Why was there no effective armoured power to strike back against the German thrust? Previous chapters of this book give the answer.

APPENDIX IV:
World War II Forces Newspapers

SEAC was not the first news sheet for the troops. With ever-growing British forces deployed in the Mediterranean theatre of operations and South East Asia, newspapers were a necessary morale-boosting link with home. They were not needed later on the Western Front because London newspapers were usually available. The principal papers were:

Crusader (1942 – 6): An 8th Army weekly originally edited by Australian Warwick Charlton and eventually circulated to Forces all over the Mediterranean.

Union Jack (1943 – 6): First published in Algiers with editions three times weekly, it moved on with invading armies to be printed in various Italian centres as a daily. In charge was Hugh Cudlipp and contributers included Cassandra (Bill Connor), sports columnist Peter Wilson, and Jon (John Jones) who drew the Two Types cartoons about a pair of eccentric Desert Rats and post-war worked with distinction for the *News Chronicle* and *Daily Mail*.

SEAC (1944 – 6): The publication editor-in-chief Frank Owen considered his 'finest hour' (see Chapters 10 – 12).

APPENDIX V:

London Saints and Sinners Club 1960

Chairman: Frank Owen. Vice-chairman: Sir Ronald Howe, Billy Butlin. Members included: Ches Allen, Tom Arnold, Arthur Askey, Douglas Bader, Sir Beverley Baxter, Lord Boothby, Sir David Bowes-Lyon, Arthur Christiansen, Lord Evans, Bud Flanagan, Charles Forte, Percy Hoskins, Jack Hylton, Cecil Moores, Frank More O'Farrell, Val Parnell, Sir Stanley Rous, Sir Malcolm Sargent, Christopher Soames, Jack Solomons, Sir Miles Thomas, Jack Train.

BIBLIOGRAPHY

BOOKS BY FRANK OWEN

Red Rainbow (novel by Owen & Cemlyn Jones) 1931
His Was the Kingdom (Abdication history
   by Owen & R J Thompson) 1937
Guilty Men (by Owen, Michael Foot
   & Peter Howard). 1938
The Three Dictators 1940
Our Ally China. 1942
The Campaign in Burma (Government publication) 1946
Tempestuous Journey (Life of Lloyd George) 1954
The Eddie Chapman Story. 1956
Peron: His Rise and Fall. 1957
The Fall of Singapore 1960

HISTORIES, BIOGRAPHIES ETC

Mark Amory (ed.): The Letters of Ann Fleming (Collins Harvill, 1985)
Arthur H Booth: British Hustings 1924 – 50 (Muller, 1956)
Anne Chisholm & Michael Davie: Beaverbrook (Hutchinson, 1992)
Raymond Callaghan: Burma 1942 – 5 (Davis Poynter, 1980)
John Campbell: Nye Bevan and the Mirage of British Socialism (Weidenfeld & Nicholson, 1987)
Arthur Christiansen: Headlines All My Life (Heinemann, 1961)
Geoffrey Cox: Countdown to War (Williams Kimber, 1988)
Hugh Cudlipp: Publish and Be Damned (Dakers, 1953)
Michael Foot: Aneurin Bevan, Vol I (McGibbon & Key, 1962)
Debts of Honour (Davis Poynter, 1980)
Dictionary of National Biography 1971 – 80 (pages 646 – 8)
Robert Hewison: Under Siege (Quartet Books, 1979)
Peter Howard: Beaverbrook (Hutchinson, 1964)
Philip Gibbs: The Street of Adventure (1909)
Cecil King: With Malice Toward None (Sidgwick & Jackson, 1970)
Ronald Lewin: Slim, the Standardbearer (Lee Cooper, 1976)
David Low: Europe Since Versailles (Penguin, 1940)
John Masters: The Road Past Mandalay (London, 1961).
Edgar Mowrer: Germany Puts the Clock Back (Penguin, 1938)
Robert Shepherd: A Class Divided (Macmillan, 1988)
Robert Skidelsky: Oswald Mosley (Papermac, 1981)

A J P Taylor: Beaverbrook (Hamish Hamilton, 1972)
John Terraine: The Life and Times of Lord Mountbatten (Hutchinson, 1968)
Walter Theimer: Penguin Political Dictionary (1939)
George Malcolm Thomson: Lord Castlerosse (Weidenfeld & Nicholson, 1973)
John Trythall: Boney Fuller, the Intellectual General (Cassell, 1977)
Kenneth Young: Churchill and Beaverbrook (Eyre & Spottiswoode, 1966)
Trevor Wignall: Never a Dull Moment (Hutchinson, 1940)
Philip Ziegler: Mountbatten (Collins, 1985)

ARTICLES

Anon: Feature (Cavalcade, March 6, 1937)
Victor Brodsky: Frank Owen – Youth Triumphant (World's Press News, Dec 1, 1938)
Tom Driberg: Editor to the 14th Army (Leader, Jan 27, 1945)
Ludovic Kennedy: Beaverbrook's Vendetta (The Listener, Nov 20, 1980)

OBITUARIES: The Times, Daily Telegraph, Evening Standard (by Michael Foot)

NEWSPAPERS: Daily Express, Daily Mail, Evening Standard, South Wales Argus (Newport), Hereford Journal, Hereford Times, SEAC.

PICTURE SOURCES: Associated Newspapers, Pages 25,40, 113, 115. Express Newspapers, p 33. Derek Evans, frontispiece, pages 57, 63, 137, 140–1, 12. Anna Phillips, pages 71, 123, 151. John Butler p 13. Reg Edwards, p 129. John Tebbut p 22–3.

INDEX